More Praise for *Leading So People Will Follow*

"A fresh, approachable, and compelling guide for improving one's leadership profile. It is a very worthy read."

> —Douglas R. Conant, retired president and CEO, Campbell Soup Company; *New York Times* best-selling author of *TouchPoints: Creating Powerful Leadership Connections in the Smallest of Moments*

✳ ✳ ✳

"For over a decade I've worked with Erika and her colleagues, and they've consistently helped us get ready and stay ready for the future. In *Leading So People Will Follow*, she gives all leaders the tools to craft a desired future in their own lives and work."

> —Benita Fitzgerald Mosley, chief of sport performance, USA Track & Field

✳ ✳ ✳

"In *Leading So People Will Follow*, Erika has captured much of what has made our work with her so valuable over the years. She answers the complex question of what it takes to lead well, in an engaging, practical, and inspiring way."

> —Dawn Ostroff, president, Condé Nast Entertainment Group

LEADING
SO PEOPLE WILL
FOLLOW

LEADING
SO PEOPLE WILL
FOLLOW

Erika Andersen

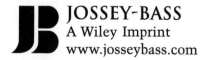

JOSSEY-BASS
A Wiley Imprint
www.josseybass.com

Jacket design by Adrian Morgan
Author photo by Dion Ogust
Cover art © Mike Truchon Shutterstock

Published by Jossey-Bass
A Wiley Imprint
One Montgomery Street, Suite 1200, San Francisco, CA 94104-4594—www.josseybass.com

Jossey-Bass books and products are available through most bookstores. To contact Jossey-Bass directly call our Customer Care Department within the U.S. at 800-956-7739, outside the U.S. at 317-572-3986, or fax 317-572-4002.

Wiley publishes in a variety of print and electronic formats and by print-on-demand. Some material included with standard print versions of this book may not be included in e-books or in print-on-demand. If this book refers to media such as a CD or DVD that is not included in the version you purchased, you may download this material at http://booksupport.wiley.com. For more information about Wiley products, visit www.wiley.com.

Library of Congress Cataloging-in-Publication Data

Andersen, Erika.
    Leading so people will follow / Erika Andersen. – 1st ed.
        p. cm.
    Includes index.
    ISBN 978-1-118-37987-5 (cloth); ISBN 978-1-118-43169-6 (ebk.); ISBN 978-1-118-43170-2 (ebk.); ISBN 978-1-118-43168-9 (ebk.)
    1. Leadership.   I. Title.
    HD57.7.A524 2012
    658.4'092–dc23

2012027909

Printed in the United States of America
FIRST EDITION

HB Printing   10 9 8 7 6 5 4 3 2 1

To my beloved bear and our FGL

Contents

LEADING
SO PEOPLE WILL
FOLLOW

ONE

The Longing for Good Leaders

We want good leaders. In fact, we crave good leaders. We're hungry for good, worthy, followable leaders in every part of our lives.

You can see it in our very public cynicism about and hanging-out-to-dry of all the leaders who fall short of our expectations. You can hear it in our hopeful, almost mythic, recounting of tales of those leaders we think/feel/believe just might be great.

We have a deeply wired-in need for leaders who will guide us well and safely; who care more about the success of the enterprise than about their own comfort; who call out our best and take full advantage of who we are. And we long to be that kind of leader as well—to evoke that *I'm with you—let's go!* response from those who work with and for us.

I've come to believe that this longing for good leaders is an ancient, primal group survival mechanism. Until recently, if you chose badly in terms of who you decided to follow, you and your family and friends were likely to die: to starve to death, be overrun by invaders, fall into violent lawlessness. And although the stakes aren't as high these days (generally), our wiring hasn't really changed.

This book offers a window into what those core timeless attributes are, why they are so essential to us, and, perhaps most important, how to develop these attributes in yourself. How to become the leader people will follow, so that together you can build strong teams and companies that will survive and thrive through the modern business version of famine and invasions.

So how did I crack the code?

In the mid-1990s, I was balancing two very important things (this may resonate for many of you): my family and my business. I had young children, and the consulting firm I had founded in 1990 was starting to take off. I spent most days observing and working with leaders in client companies and most evenings reading bedtime stories.

I started to notice something very interesting in my client organizations. Often the person who was the appointed leader was not the person others looked to for direction and reassurance. In one meeting this was so blatantly the case that I wondered that others didn't notice; the CEO would say something, and most of the folks attending the meeting would quickly glance at the CFO to note his reaction. They clearly, though perhaps unconsciously, were treating the CFO as their actual leader, even though the CEO was the official leader.

What is it, I started to wonder, *that makes someone willing to consider one person his or her leader but not another?*

At the same time, as I was reading story after story to my kids, I began to notice that many of the tales were about someone overcoming adversity to become a worthy leader. In fact, the more I read, the more I noticed a pattern: the poor lad (almost always a lad versus a lass, but we'll overlook that for the moment), generally the youngest and least impressive of three brothers, makes his way through a very specific and predictable series of trials. And in the process, he develops or reveals a core set of personal attributes that allow him to save the princess and become the wise and just ruler by the end of the tale.

Many of the stories my daughter and son loved best were from a series of books published in the early twentieth century that included fairy stories and folktales from all over the world. As I read them, I noticed that this pattern of attributes essential to becoming a leader was remarkably consistent across time and culture. It seemed to me that I had stumbled on an archetype. So as I read and continued to look for the common elements, I began to think about why this should be so—why human beings would have a built-in archetype for the qualities to look for in a leader.

It occurred to me that until a few hundred years ago, the goal of most collections of people (villages, tribes, ethnic or religious groups) was much more clearly defined and compelling than those of today's organizations. Groups of human beings came together to survive, literally, against human enemies and the challenges of nature. The job of the leader was to help the people stay alive. Once that was assured, it was also hoped that he or she would make decisions that allowed life to be reasonably pleasant, that is, free enough from the fear of capture or death (or both) to allow the creation of some sort of family and spiritual life. The tribe would only put its fate in the hands of a chieftain who had proven his worth and fitness to lead; the stakes were too high to trust someone ill equipped to handle the tasks of leadership. Most often in prefeudal cultures, leadership was not hereditary; leaders were chosen on the basis of demonstrated prowess in hunting, in council, in war.

Today most of us are far safer from the threat of starvation or war than were our ancestors. But thousands of years of conditioning don't evaporate within a few hundred years. Gun control, antibiotics, credit cards, and peace accords between major nations don't take away our deeply felt need for worthy chieftains.

So when someone who is put in the leader seat doesn't demonstrate the leadership qualities for which human beings have a kind of built-in radar, that person is unlikely to be effective as a leader. If the people are tentative in their acceptance of the leader, if that person doesn't satisfy their "leader hunger," they are less likely to offer their commitment and support, and it's more difficult for that person to guide the organization to success.

As I thought about these things, I continued to observe my clients and their interactions with one another. Time and again, I watched as people chose their real leaders quietly, without a conscious or verbalized selection process. This is not to say that the process was invisible

3

or arbitrary. It was relatively easy to observe once I started noticing it, and there was definitely a pattern to it. As I began to pull out the key attributes of leadership from the folktales I was reading, I noticed over and over that people seemed willing to fully accept someone as their leader, and commit to being a true member of that person's team, only when he or she demonstrated these attributes.

Naming the Elements

I began to get excited: I felt if I could clarify these archetypal elements and translate them into today's organizational reality, I would have a tool that could be dramatically helpful to people wanting to become more effective leaders: *wanting to become a leader that others would follow*.

After much observation and reflection, I felt I had come to a clear way to describe what I was reading about and understanding. I decided to test out the model with a real-life leader, someone who was not only the designated leader but to whom others clearly looked as the person who "felt like" the leader as well. I shared with him what I've just told you, and then I explained the six leadership attributes that had emerged in my research as the key components of the leadership archetype. He listened carefully and immediately began to use the model. His first response was, "So, Eileen [one of his senior team members] has the first three elements, but I'm not sure about the last three. I bet that's what's getting in her way. And we definitely have to work on the first one with Larry. And I think I'm pretty good on all of them except the third. How would I work on that?"

I was excited. The fact that he immediately, without question or confusion, began to apply the attributes to real leaders in his organization, and to himself, argued to me that I had indeed stumbled onto something primal, that I had identified those attributes that resonate in our "looking-for-leaders DNA."

Fast-Forward

Now it's almost fifteen years later. My children are adults, soon to be reading bedtime stories to their own children. My colleagues and I at Proteus International now use this "leading" model to help people at every level in organizations think and behave as leaders. We've found that learning these six attributes gives people a useful, practical framework for self-reflection and growth. And it helps them build more productive teams and organizations by becoming the leader who provides a strong, safe point around which people's hopes and efforts can coalesce. We've taught the model to young men and women in their first "leader" jobs, and we've used it to coach CEOs. It makes immediate logical and intuitive sense to most people, and it seems to be almost universally helpful as a tool for their leadership growth.

I hope this book will provide you with a simple, immediately applicable approach to looking at yourself as a leader with fresh eyes and that it will then guide you in deciding what you need to do to become the sort of leader who is truly given the chance to lead. I'll approach our time together as I would if I were coaching you one-on-one: I'll share stories and examples, provide a framework for thinking, encourage you to self-assess, and offer self-directed activities to help you discover and strengthen each of these six attributes in yourself. This model can help you understand what it takes to be a leader others will gladly follow and then offers you guidance to develop those characteristics in yourself.

If you want to lead, I'm offering you a set of tools to be the kind of leader people long for—one who can partner with and guide them past all of the modern trolls and monsters you'll encounter, so that you can find your own twenty-first-century happy endings.

On to the journey!

TWO

Firesides and Folktales

Once upon a time . . .

Even now, as adults, there's something in most of us that perks up and starts to listen when we hear those words. We love stories. And stories have always served important functions for us. They bring us together and reinforce our sense of community. They engage, amuse, enthrall, and titillate. And they teach: throughout history, before most people could read and write, stories, told by firesides and in village gatherings, were the mechanism by which we handed down laws and values, religions and taboos, knowledge and wisdom.

Think of stories as the cultural DNA of a preliterate society. The stories of a group of people provided a map that, if followed, would guide someone to be a successful member of that group.

And over the centuries, some of those maps seem to have transcended culture and geography to offer guidance for being successful humans. This seems especially true for one type of story: the hero's tale. Joseph Campbell explored this theme in religious mythology with brilliance and depth in his *Hero with a Thousand Faces*, and I'm indebted to his work. However, in exploring these story maps for clues to the characteristics that define leadership, I looked to more humble sources: the folktales and fairy tales of many cultures. Campbell's work focused on our highest aspirations: what we expect of gods and godlike heroes. I wanted to know something more practical: how folktales tell us what to look for and accept in those who lead us day-to-day.

Think of folktales as maps of success—how to live as safely and happily as possible, how to avoid making fatal mistakes of belief or action. Until recently in our history, choosing a leader was a life-or-death decision. A good leader could guide you to find food, overcome enemies, and keep peace within the society. A bad leader could lead you into starvation or to death through war or lawlessness. And although the stakes may not be as high today, we're still wired to accept as leaders only those who line up with our centuries-old map of leadership attributes.

Drawing the Map

By finding and extracting these leader maps, I reasoned, I could learn not only what people look for in leaders but the corollary of that: what it takes to be the kind of leader whom others would follow. And after reading hundreds of leader stories from all over the world, here's what I discovered:

The acknowledged leader is

- Farsighted
- Passionate
- Courageous
- Wise
- Generous
- Trustworthy

Here's a quick overview of the essence of each of these characteristics.

In leader folktales, the leader-to-be can see beyond his current situation (young, poor, despised) to his ultimate goal (save his father, win the princess, kill the monster) and can express that vision in a compelling and inclusive way, especially to those whose help he needs to achieve it. He can hold to that vision and share it clearly even when others lose sight of it, believe it's impossible, or ridicule him for trying. He is *farsighted*.

Moreover, the leader-in-training doesn't just go through the motions. He is deeply committed to his quest, with his every action directed toward achieving it. Nothing dissuades him, even the inevitable setbacks and disappointments attendant on any quest. He may not be loud about it, but he is relentless. He is *passionate*.

Throughout the story, he is confronted with difficult situations. He may be afraid and lonely; he may feel like running away, longing for the comfort and safety of home. He often faces situations that are particularly trying for him personally. But he doesn't turn aside; he doesn't (unlike his brothers or others who attempt the same journey) make the safe and easy choices. He doesn't wimp out and take the path of least resistance. He is *courageous*.

He's not a cardboard action hero, though. His brain is tested, and he must be able to learn from his mistakes. In many versions of the story, he doesn't initially follow the advice given him ("don't look back"; "don't let go"; "don't touch this or that on your way out"), and his mistakes create more complexity and danger. The next time a similar situation arises, though, he behaves differently and succeeds at his task. He doesn't deny or whine or blame; he improves. He also often comes up with clever solutions to seemingly insoluble problems. Finally, he uses his powers of discrimination to think through difficult choices and arrive at the best and most moral solution (for example, long-term happiness versus current riches; the greater good versus pure self-interest). He is thoughtful, appropriately humble, clear-headed, and curious. He is *wise*.

Along the way, the future leader meets people or creatures in need, and he helps them or shares with them. He does so even though his own supplies are low, and even though helping them takes him out of his way or slows him down. In some versions of the story, he has to sacrifice his life for those he loves or to whom he owes his loyalty (this always turns out okay in the end). And later, when he is king, his people are prosperous and happy because he rules with an open hand. The leader is not stingy, miserly, or selfish. He is *generous*.

Finally, and perhaps most important, his word is his bond. If he tells his dying father that he will find the magic potion to cure him, you know that he will. If he tells the princess that he will come back to marry her, she can send out the invitations. When some creature says to him, "If I help you, boy, you must free me," you know the creature is as good as free. The hero does not equivocate or exaggerate. He is *trustworthy*.

This tale survives and thrives in almost infinite permutations because it is satisfying, and it feels right to us. We are hardwired to expect our chieftains to be farsighted, passionate, courageous, wise, generous, and trustworthy. If we don't see these qualities clearly demonstrated, we won't follow wholeheartedly; it feels dangerous to do so.

Of course, we're not entirely doctrinaire about this; we know that no real, living leader is perfect. If we are asked to follow someone who has four or five of these qualities, we will do it, all the while watching to see if he or she is working to add the missing or less developed qualities.

What About You?

Before we go on, I encourage you to take a few moments to reflect on your own current state as a leader:

1. Reread "Drawing the Map" for each of the six characteristics.
2. Reflect on your own current behavior (versus how you'd like to behave) relative to that characteristic.
3. Assess yourself as a leader below, noting whether you feel a characteristic is currently a growth area for you (you don't demonstrate this characteristic consistently), a strength (you demonstrate it consistently), or a key strength (you clearly exemplify it and demonstrate it almost always).

Leader Attribute	Self-Assessment
Farsighted	(1) Growth area (2) Strength (3) Key strength
Passionate	(1) Growth area (2) Strength (3) Key strength
Courageous	(1) Growth area (2) Strength (3) Key strength
Wise	(1) Growth area (2) Strength (3) Key strength
Generous	(1) Growth area (2) Strength (3) Key strength
Trustworthy	(1) Growth area (2) Strength (3) Key strength

I'll ask you to refer to and expand on this self-assessment and use it in support of your own growth throughout this book.

Making This Real

You may be asking (I hope you're asking!), *How can I make this real and practical for myself?* That's my job in this book. First, I'll share with you a composite folktale, one that demonstrates these six hardwired leadership attributes, so you can get a sense of these qualities as they live in their natural habitat of the fairy tale. It will almost certainly seem familiar to you, reminding you of stories you read or were told as a child—or the ones you read to your children.

Then I devote one chapter to each of the six characteristics, first pulling out the part of the story that most directly speaks to this quality, then discussing examples of the quality (or its lack) in leaders with whom I've had the pleasure to work over the past decade. In each of these chapters, I share a handful of key behaviors that exemplify this quality and provide practical ideas and guidelines for you to build the behaviors in your own life as a leader.

After exploring all six behaviors, I offer additional insights and support systems for becoming the acknowledged leader.

One disclaimer before I tell you the story: I've used the traditional form of boy-saves-princess, mainly to connect this in your mind with the folktales and fairy tales you read or had read to you as a child. (I considered reversing the genders of the protagonists at one point, but it seemed contrived.) Nevertheless, think of this as a metaphor. It could just as easily have been girl-saves-prince (or, for that matter, boy-saves-prince or girl-saves-princess). You'll see that half the real-life followable leaders I use as examples throughout the book are women. These leader attributes are core, and we've found they resonate across time, culture, race, and gender.

Now, on to our folktale.

Gather 'round, and I'll tell you a story.

Once upon a time, there lived in a small village at the end of the world a merchant and his three sons. Sadly, the boys' mother had died when the youngest was only a babe, and the father had raised the boys alone. His business dealings prospered, and the older two sons became fine young men, tall and well built, their clothing and horses the envy of all their peers. The third son was thought something of a simpleton and generally stayed at home, helping his father or dreaming by the fire.

One day, messengers of the king arrived. They dismounted in the town square and blew a fanfare on their great horns. The villagers assembled, murmuring. One of the messengers read aloud from an ornate scroll:

> By the order of his majesty the king and her majesty the queen, be it known that her royal highness the princess, their only child, has been stolen away and cruelly imprisoned by the most evil sorcerer in the land. He holds her on the highest peak of the tallest mountain, which he has turned into purest glass, so that the king's men are unable to rescue her.
>
> His majesty thus declares he will give her hand in marriage and the future kingship to that brave man who can save her and return her unharmed to her royal parents.

With that, the messengers turned their mounts and galloped away to spread their message throughout the kingdom. The villagers all began to talk at once. The two older brothers looked at one another and raced home. They burst into the house, where their father was working on his accounts and their younger brother, smudged with soot, was sweeping out the fireplace. Talking loudly over each other, the brothers relayed the royal message and asked for their father's blessing to travel to the highest mountain and rescue the princess.

"I think I should be allowed to try first, Father," said the eldest son, pushing his brother aside. "I am the eldest and bravest, and therefore have the best chance to succeed and bring honor to our family."

"But I am far cleverer," replied the second son, jostling past his brother. "You know that's true, Father; you've said it yourself." His frown was petulant. "I don't know why my brother should have first try just for being older!"

The old merchant looked at his youngest son, who had stopped his work and was simply listening. "And you?" he asked gently. "Do you also want to go?"

The youngest son looked at his brothers and rubbed his chin, leaving a streak of grime. "No, Father, let them try," he said simply.

"Very well," said the merchant. He turned back to the older brothers. "But you must go together, to help and support each other along the way." He handed each of them a small bag of gold for their journey and gave them his blessing.

Early the next morning, the older brothers set off in their best clothes, capes flowing, boots polished, every buckle of their horses' tack sparkling in the sun. Spirits high, they waved a jaunty good-bye to their father and galloped down the road toward the distant mountain, racing each other for pride of place.

Some hours later, hot, tired, and dusty, the brothers had taken off their fine cloaks and brocaded tunics. Sweat ran in rivulets down their faces, and their shirts stuck to their backs. Their fine horses had slowed to a plodding walk. Unused to long hours in the saddle, the brothers found themselves sore and ill tempered.

At a bend in the road, they spied a well, cool and shady beneath its thatched roof. Both dismounted in relief, rushing to grab the tin ladle sitting on the well's stone lip. In their jostling, the ladle fell into the well and sank. Loudly blaming each other, the brothers bent over to drink directly from the well but found the water just out of their reach.

Suddenly an ancient woman spoke from the far side of the well. They had not noticed her; she was small and wrinkled, her skin and clothing the color of leaf and grass. She leaned upon a crooked stick. "Have you a coin for an old woman?" she asked in a thin voice, holding out a tiny clawlike hand.

"Off with you, crone," snapped the eldest brother. "We have better things to do than give you money you have not earned."

"Then have you bread to share with a poor old woman?" she asked, still holding out her hand.

The second brother flapped his velvet cap at her. "Be off, we say!"

"So be it," said the old woman, her voice suddenly much stronger. The brothers watched wide-eyed as the she grew and changed, becoming tall and young, her beautiful face angry. She raised her stick, now straight and shining, and struck the older brother, tumbling him head over heels into the well, where he sank like the tin ladle before him.

The second brother jumped back, terrified. He leaped onto his horse and rode away, whipping his steed to its fastest gallop. He rode and rode until, dropping from exhaustion, he came upon a small inn almost hidden in the woods. Tumbling from his horse, he stumbled to the door and knocked upon it. It opened at once to show a strange man, as wide as he was tall, with deeply set glittering eyes. Dense furlike hair covered his face and body.

"Yes?" the creature said gruffly.

"I want food and wine, my man, as well as a wash and a bed," the second brother demanded. "Your best," he added, trying to regain his haughty demeanor. He jingled his gold purse in the man's face.

The creature grinned fiercely. "Please, come in," he said, stepping back and gesturing with his huge hand. The second brother felt a moment of hesitation—the man was so strange and the interior of the inn so dim and noisome—but his exhaustion and hunger won out, and he stepped through the doorway. The heavy door closed behind him and never opened again.

Months passed, and the merchant and his remaining son listened for any news of the older sons. Travelers to the village brought many tales of young men from all over the kingdom who had tried every clever trick, every feat of strength and bravery to scale the mountain and free the princess, but none had succeeded. No one carried word of the older brothers.

Finally, one day, the youngest son came to his father. He had washed his face and hands and put on his best clothes, simple but clean. Because he had no horse, his few belongings were bound up in a pack upon his back.

"I believe it's time for me to go, Father," he said. "The princess still needs to be rescued, and now I fear for my brothers as well."

"Are you sure, my son?" asked his father, who had aged mightily and whose fortunes had turned as he worried for his sons. "I cannot prepare you for this journey as I did your brothers; I have only a few silver coins for you instead of the gold purses I gave to them."

"No matter, Father," his son replied. "I will go as I am."

The merchant blessed his son with tears in his eyes, and the lad set off.

He walked steadily all day, stopping at the hottest hour to rest beneath the shade of a spreading tree, drinking sparingly of his water and eating the brown bread he had brought with him. Late in the evening, the boy came to the same well his brothers had found so many months before. He saw the tin ladle on the lip of the well and dipped it into the water to drink and bathe his dusty face and hands.

Just then, the same ancient crone stepped from the dusky shadows, leaning on her gnarled stick. "Have you a coin for an old woman?" she asked in her thin voice, holding out her wrinkled hand.

"Yes, certainly," said the youngest brother, dipping into his purse and selecting a small silver coin. "It's not much, but you're welcome to it."

She took the coin and hid it in the folds of her ragged gown. "And have you bread to share with a poor old woman?" she asked, holding out her hand again.

"Yes, and you are welcome to it too," said the boy, breaking off and handing to her a chunk of his simple brown bread.

"So be it," said the old woman, her voice stronger. The youngest brother watched, amazed, as the old woman grew and changed, becoming young and beautiful, her face kind. Raising her stick, now straight and shining, she touched the lip of the well.

The water in the well bubbled, and up came the eldest brother, drowned. Crying out, the boy pulled him from the well and laid him on the ground. The faery-woman said, "With your open heart, you have saved your brother," and touched the dead brother's forehead with her stick. The older lad coughed and began to breathe, but his eyes remained shut, his face pale.

"Do not be concerned," the faery-woman continued. "He will recover, and I will send him home safe to your father." She reached into her golden dress and pulled out the boy's coin, now shining with faery light. She placed the coin into his hand and said, "Put this safe upon your person. When you need me, rub it between your thumb and forefinger, and I will come to you." And with that, she and the older brother disappeared.

The boy set off again, and late the next afternoon he came upon the same small inn his brother had found. With the hope of a bed and a hot meal, he knocked on the door.

The huge, hairy man-creature opened the door and smiled his feral smile. "Yes?" he asked.

Not at all liking what he saw, the boy asked mildly and respectfully, "Good sir, have you a stable you need cleaned or animals fed? I am a poor traveler and will work for my food." He kept his purse, and especially his shining coin, well hidden.

"Are you sure you won't come in?" wheedled the creature. "I have hot food and a soft bed for only a few coins."

"Oh no," the boy replied. "Such things are far too good for me. Cold food and hay to sleep on are all I need."

"Have it your way, then," the creature growled. "Clean the stable and feed and water my horses, and you can eat of the cheese and bread you'll find there and sleep in the hayloft." He started to close the door, but all of a sudden stopped and turned fiercely. "But don't mess about with my birds, boy. You'll see pretty birds in cages in the stables; leave them be, or regret it." The lad nodded, and the creature slammed the heavy door.

As he entered the stables, the boy saw many fine horses along one side and beautiful cages filled with colorful birds along the other. With a shock, he recognized his brother's big roan horse partway down the aisle. At the same time, one of the birds flew wildly to the edge of its cage and began to beat its wings against the bars.

The youngest brother ran to the cage. "Is it you, brother?" he asked. The bird dipped its beak as if nodding. The boy reached out for the cage's latch, but stopped the moment before his hand touched the ornate metal, remembering the beast-man's words.

Instead, he pulled the faery's shining coin from his pocket and rubbed it. The faery-woman appeared at once on a sweet breeze. The boy explained the situation, and she touched the cages with her shining staff. The latches fell apart, and all the birds flew out and away, arrowing silently through the stable's windows to freedom. The brother-bird flew out too, landing on his younger brother's shoulder and nibbling his ear affectionately with its beak. The younger lad thanked the faery, bowing low. She inclined her head and disappeared. He quickly found his brother's tack, saddled his horse, and wrapped rags around the beast's hooves to muffle their sound. He rode quietly out of the stable and into the woods, his brother-bird on his shoulder.

They slept deep in the woods that night, and in the morning the youngest son was overjoyed to see that his brother had regained his human form. They embraced, and the middle brother implored him, "Oh, little brother, let us go home and live in peace with our father. We've barely begun our journey, and look at the dreadful things that have happened already."

The younger brother replied, "You are welcome to go home. However, the princess is still held on her lonely mountaintop, and someone must save her, so I will continue."

The middle brother shook his head. "Little brother, think of all those smarter, braver, and stronger than you who have failed. Come back to our father's house with me."

"That's as may be," replied the younger son, "but I must do what I can do."

Finally, the middle brother pulled at his arm. "Be reasonable, little brother! Come back to the fireside; you are being foolish."

The lad smiled and repeated, "That's as may be, but still, I must do what I can do."

The middle brother embraced him and turned for home, shaking his head.

After many days of traveling, the younger brother found himself in the mountains and came to a narrow pass between high cliffs. As he walked his horse carefully through the divide, he was suddenly surrounded by small, strange men. Half the size of a normal man, with pale faces and long ears, they all carried sharp little pikes or deadly looking dart blowers.

"You trespass on our land," said one, clearly the leader, in a high, fierce voice. "Why should we not kill and eat you now?"

"Because then you would not hear my story," said the young man. "And it is a very good story."

The small men all looked at one another. "Very good?" asked the leader.

"Very good indeed."

The next he knew, he was sitting before their fire, a tender roasted joint of meat in his hand, telling them of his quest, of the beautiful princess held captive on the mountain, of all the brave and strong young men who had tried and failed to save her, of her royal parents wasting away with grief in their castle. He shared with them how he hoped to find a way to save the princess and bring joy to all the people.

By the end of his tale, the fierce little men were enthralled. The leader struck his shield upon the ground. "A very, very good story," he said stoutly. Then he jumped to his feet, his pike held over his head. "We will come too!" he cried. "We will support you in your quest to save the princess!" All the other little men also jumped to their feet and began dancing around the fire, shouting, "We will save the princess, save the princess!"

Soon enough the youngest son and his army of little men found themselves at the base of the glass mountain. The king's subjects had long since given up the effort, and only foreign princes with their retinues and powerful horses were vying to save the princess. Flags flew over their colorful silk tents, and a town of sorts had grown around them, complete with food sellers, camp followers, and spectators. It was a festive scene. Although the youngest brother's tiny army earned him some strange looks, for the most part everyone ignored the slender lad in simple clothing on his brother's tired horse.

After investigating the mountain (and watching one fine prince on his war horse slide ingloriously down the slope), they found a place to camp and gathered around a hastily built fire to decide their course of action.

"We have conferred," said the leader of the little men. "I can get you to the top of the mountain. But it will be—frightening."

The lad swallowed, his throat dry. "Tell me," he said.

"You've seen our dart blowers," the leader went on, gesturing at his weapon, "but you've not seen us use them. They have a strong magic."

He pulled a small bag from his tunic and hefted it in one hand. "We have a dust that can shrink you small enough to fit into my blower. And I can blow you on a breath of magic to the top of the mountain, where you will land softly and regain your normal size."

The boy sat silently thinking. He had always been smaller than his brothers, smaller than the other boys in the village. And the idea of being even smaller, smaller than an almond, was truly terrifying to him. What if he didn't return to normal? What if he didn't land softly and was crushed on the mountaintop? What if . . . ?

But then he took a deep breath: "I will do it. Let's rise at dawn, before the others, so the way is clear." All the little men nodded solemnly and lay down to sleep.

Terrifying though it was, all happened as the little man had promised, and the youngest brother found himself on the peak of the mountain, back to his normal size, just as the sun was rising. He stood and looked about, and there before him was the captive princess, chained to a large flat rock. Her face in sleep was both beautiful and noble, her body strong and graceful, and he fell in love with her as he stood watching.

She opened her eyes and looked directly into his, her gaze filled with intelligence and joy. "I thank you for coming to me," she said simply.

"Princess," he said respectfully, bowing.

She held up her chained hands. "The sorcerer has the key, and he has told me that he will unlock my bonds only if a fully honest man comes to save me. Are you that man?"

"I hope so," said the lad.

Suddenly, in a flash of lightning, the sorcerer appeared, tall and skeletally thin, his skin greenish and his eyes glittering black, wrapped in a long, dark cloak that gleamed and moved disturbingly.

"At last, a worthy suitor," he said, his voice deep and echoing. "Are you a prince, lad?"

"No," the boy said simply.

"No?" the sorcerer raised an eyebrow. "No royal blood at all? Why on earth would I release this beautiful prize to a commoner?"

The lad looked briefly at the princess, so lovely and strong, so solemn and bright, and thought perhaps he could say he had just a bit of royal blood, if that would sway the sorcerer to his cause.

He sighed. "No. No royal blood at all."

To the lad's astonishment, the sorcerer laughed aloud. "Good for you, boy," he said, and waved his hand.

In that moment, the youngest brother and the princess found themselves transported to the king's throne room, where the grateful king and queen ran to embrace their daughter, laughing and crying. The boy stood back a little shyly, until the princess grasped his hand and pulled him forward, telling her parents how he had rescued her and letting them know that she would be happy to fulfill her father's promise to marry him and rule together.

The king and queen agreed at once. The princess and the youngest brother were married. The father, the much-chastened brothers, the little men, and even the faery-woman came to the wedding and celebrated his good fortune. The princess and the lad were glad together, and when the old king and queen died after long and happy lives, the princess and the youngest-brother-turned-king ruled with kindness, justice, and joy.

And they all lived happily ever after, of course.

Now we'll take the story apart and focus on each of the six leader attributes. Before we get started, though, here are some ideas about how to make the most of our journey together through this book.

First, I encourage you to read the rest of the book in whatever way works best for you. The next six chapters focus on the six leadership qualities.

Every chapter examines one of the attributes, explaining it in more depth and with real-life examples and then breaking it down into five key behaviors so you can see more clearly what you'll need to do, practically and behaviorally, to develop that quality. I've offered specific activities to help you develop each of the behaviors within the attributes, which you'll find in sections labeled "Try It."

You may prefer to read straight through the book, skipping over the activities to come back to later. Or you might want to go directly to the chapters that cover the attributes where you feel you need the most improvement, focusing on the behaviors and the associated activities you believe will be most helpful to you. Then again, you might like to skim until something catches your eye or resonates for you, then read and try out that part.

Whatever works for you is fine by me. I've written this for you as I would for any leader I'm coaching, and I've put in it the essential information and support that I thought you would find most useful in developing these leader attributes. My job is to offer these skills and insights as clearly and engagingly as possible; yours is to take what's most useful for you in the way that suits you best.

One other aspect of this book I'd like to share with you at this point: the next chapter, "Farsighted," is somewhat longer than the following ones. That's because I introduce in it, and explain in detail, some skills and concepts that are fundamental to being the kind of leader others will follow. These skills will help you develop your ability to be farsighted, and they will also support you in developing the other leader attributes as well. I intend to give you a foundation in these skills in this chapter and then build on that foundation in subsequent chapters.

Let's get started. I want to help you find your own happily ever after—as a truly accepted, fully followable leader.

THREE

Farsighted

The next he knew, he was sitting before their fire, a tender roasted joint of meat in his hand, telling them of his quest, of the beautiful princess held captive on the mountain, of all the brave and strong young men who had tried and failed to save her, of her royal parents wasting away with grief in their castle. He shared with them how he hoped to find a way to save the princess and bring joy to all the people.

By the end of his tale, the fierce little men were enthralled. The leader struck his shield upon the ground. "A very, very good story," he said stoutly. Then he jumped to his feet, his pike held over his head. "We will come too!" he cried. "We will support you in your quest to save the princess!" All the other little men also jumped to their feet and began dancing around the fire, shouting, "We will save the princess, save the princess!"

Bonnie Hammer is tiny. She stands before the Universal Cable Production Studios team, forty-some people who together have created some of the most successful cable television shows of the past few years—*Warehouse 13*, *Royal Pains*, and *Psych* among them—and those in the back rows have to sit up straight to see her. This is the first time in the studio's brief history that the whole group has come together to focus on their vision for the studio's future and plan how to get there.

Bonnie is the chairman of NBCU Cable Entertainment and Cable Studios. She's had huge success building her portfolio of businesses over the past decade, so folks in the room respect her and would be ready to listen even if she wasn't inspiring. But she is. She may be little, but her energy is infectious, and she builds a picture of how the media industry is changing and the role this group could play; of how the studio can succeed both financially and creatively in this new world. She talks about how their collaboration with each other and with all their partners both inside and outside the company will support them in creating great content for people to enjoy not only on TV but online, on their phones, in games, and on platforms and in formats yet to be invented. She describes a future of risk taking rewarded, of working hard, having fun, being pioneers.

Everyone in the room is engaged; there are smiles and nods. Watching from the side of the room, I see that at this moment, they are fully accepting her as their leader. One of her direct reports leans over to me and says, "She's really something, isn't she?"

Bonnie is farsighted. She also has the other leader qualities as well; I'm using her as an example of farsightedness because she demonstrates it particularly clearly and consistently. Over the years as I've worked with her and her teams, I've watched her again and again as she pulls people's eyes up from the ground and turns them toward the far horizon, describing a possible future and inviting people to go there with her. She shares her vision of the future in a compelling and inclusive way.

Those who work for her are genuinely inspired to be part of the future she envisions with them. And her farsightedness has powerful business results: every part of her portfolio is extremely successful. In addition to the successes of the Universal Cable Production Studio, the cable networks she oversees are among the most watched and well-regarded in the industry.

Why Farsightedness Is Important

If you have had the good fortune to have observed or worked with someone like Bonnie in your career, I'll bet it was a deeply positive and memorable experience. You may want to reflect on that person, or on Bonnie, as I explain more about how farsightedness operates and why it's important. It will help to make this quality more three-dimensional and meaningful for you as I describe it.

We are drawn to leaders who articulate a possible future in a way that speaks to us and includes us. In the excerpt of the folktale at the beginning of this chapter, the hero uses his clarity of purpose to get him out of a tight spot: by sharing with the little men his quest and the outcome he hopes for, he inspires them to join him and be part of his success. Bonnie, and other leaders like her, do the same thing: their clarity of vision and their articulation of a successful future pull people out of fear or short-sightedness and into hopefulness and a sense of purpose.

People want leaders who look beyond today. They want to have the sense there is a master plan to carry them through whatever short-term trials and tribulations arise. (*The recession! The crazy media landscape! Lions and tigers and bears, oh my!*) They look to the leader to articulate, in a compelling way, a clear and positive future state toward which they can direct their efforts. When leaders focus only on the current crisis or this quarter's numbers, it seems to us that they're more interested in maintaining the status quo or protecting themselves than in creating a successful future. They are not seen as leaders.

People also want to see that the leader's farsightedness is based on a deep sense of what's necessary, right, and good for the business and the team rather than what's simply expeditious, popular, or self-serving. We want to feel that our leaders' "far-sight" is focused on the greater good, that their vision promotes the group and not just their own selfish interests. A truly farsighted leader envisions a possible future that responds to and resonates with people's aspirations for their individual and collective success. When employees or potential employees hear about the good leader's vision, their visceral response is, "Yes, I want to go there too."

This is not to imply that the visionary leader simply goes for the easy win, the thing to which people will most easily commit. True visionaries often see possibilities where others see difficulty and dead-ends. Most people in the first decade of the twentieth century saw motorcars as a fad for the rich, a frivolous and uncertain fancy that would never replace the dependability of the horse. Henry Ford's vision of a nation where every family would have an automobile seemed laughable, impossible, and even dangerous. Only the clarity of his vision and his consistency in moving toward it brought the support from others that he needed to make his vision a reality.

This brings up a critical point about farsightedness: the leader must not only articulate her vision; she must live it. It can't be something she dusts off for quarterly staff meetings. People must witness the vision serving as the leader's compass. She must use it as a screen for strategy and action. True farsightedness in a leader is both practical and aspirational.

As it does with Bonnie and her teams, a clear and compelling vision can drive extraordinary business results. It provides a focus for people's decisions and actions, and it creates that feeling of "tribe" that most people find necessary and motivating.

This quality of leadership is especially important when the enterprise is a new one and the future is uncharted. One stunning example of this kind of farsightedness is how Steve Jobs operated at the start of Apple. When Jobs and Wozniak founded Apple Computers in 1976, the personal computer was still new and untested. Moreover, the idea that almost everyone would one day have a computer and that computers would be as accessible and easy-to-use as televisions or telephones seemed like craziness.

But then along came these two young men with exactly these ideas. And Jobs, especially, continued to articulate this possible future in a way that brought together capital, a workforce, and a marketing plan that ultimately led to the achievement of the future he envisioned thirty-five years ago.

As I said earlier and as you saw in the fairy tale, the essence of farsightedness is not only envisioning a possible successful future but also articulating it in a way that's both compelling and inclusive. *Compelling* means that it's meaningful to those who hear it, that it's attractive to them. *Inclusive* means they want to help make it happen and feel they can have an important part to play in moving toward it.

Clearly Steve Jobs was able (I encourage you to watch any of his company presentations on YouTube or at the apple.com Web site) to express his vision for the future in this way. In January 1984, when Jobs introduced the first Macintosh computer at Apple's annual shareholders' meeting, an attendee described the level of enthusiasm as "pandemonium." As the first commercially successful small computer with a graphical user interface, the Macintosh represented, and still represents, the realization of a vision that was both compelling and inclusive.

How to Be Farsighted

You may be thinking, *Okay, but how do I become more farsighted if that's not one of my strengths*? Fortunately, my colleagues and I have gotten clearer over the years on the specific behaviors that make up each of these leadership attributes. And that's good news for you, because it means you and I can spend the rest of this chapter, and part of each chapter that follows, figuring out how you can develop your own capability in each of these areas.

We start with *farsighted*. When you deconstruct this element, these are the key behaviors of which it consists:

Leaders Who Are Farsighted

1. See possible futures that are good for the enterprise
2. Articulate their vision in a compelling and inclusive way
3. Model their vision
4. See past obstacles
5. Invite others to participate in the vision

I'll explore each of these in depth and offer some ideas about how to build each one, but first, take a minute and self-assess in each of these behaviors. For each of the five "farsighted" indicators, note how well you think you do this. Use a scale of 1 to 3 to rate yourself in these indicators, where 1 is, "I don't do this consistently; it's definitely a growth area"; 2 is, "This is a strength of mine; I do it consistently"; and 3 is, "I am unusually skilled and consistent in this area; it's a key strength." Try to be as objective and honest as possible. Having a sense of where you are now in demonstrating each of these behaviors will help you take best advantage of the developmental advice I'm about to share.

#1 See Possible Futures That Are Good for the Enterprise

All of us have the capacity to be visionaries. That is, we can each imagine futures that don't yet exist. Every kid who's ever wanted a bike for Christmas does it: he or she imagines racing down the street on that shiny bike, hair streaming in the wind, sneakered feet pumping steel and rubber pedals, hands tight around the handlebars. What is that if not envisioning a hoped-for future?

Unfortunately, we can all get in the way of that capability too. We can stifle it (*I know I'll never get that bike; it just won't happen*) or we can take it too far and envision impossible outcomes (*Yes! And maybe my bike will have wings, so I can fly on it too!*)

Seeing possible futures that are good for the business requires being able to make best use of this innate human capability. You need to learn to engage your natural capacity to envision in a balanced way, neither stifling it nor being wildly unrealistic. Before I offer some guidance about how to do this, here are additional insights about how people over- and underuse their visioning capabilities.

Sometimes, as I noted, a vision for the future can be unrealistic—too much of a stretch. Generally when people come up with such unrealistic visions—bikes that fly, companies that succeed without sufficient capital—those visions are based on an inaccurate understanding of current reality, where the laws of physics make airborne bikes unlikely and the laws of the marketplace make start-up capital essential. If you start from a faulty assessment of your current situation—one that's based on wishful thinking or incomplete information—it's likely your vision won't be achievable. I see this pattern often: executives who set goals and firmly believe that they can achieve them, all the while ignoring the fact that people necessary to the accomplishment of those goals don't support them; entrepreneurs who envision their future company and are deeply committed to that vision, regardless of the fact that they lack the skills or resources to create it and have no plan to acquire them.

The sad thing is that when these pie-in-the-sky visions don't come to pass, people tend to blame others or to blame visioning itself, saying some version of, "I guess it just doesn't pay to have hopes and dreams," rather than to focus on their own faulty assessment of reality. This is one reason that, in being farsighted, it's critically important to get clear about your current reality before you move on to envisioning a possible future. Unless you can be objective about where you're starting from and what you have to work with, it's all too easy to set your sights on an unreachable outcome.

Sometimes, though, a vision sets the bar too low. By this I mean that some people undermine their visioning capacity in just the opposite way: they hesitate to envision a possible future much different from what they have now. They stifle their natural capacity to envision through self-doubt. For many years I watched a dear friend get in the way of his own success in this way. He would begin to envision a future career that appealed to him—one that he would have had the skills and resources to achieve—and before he could begin to move toward realizing his dream, he would talk himself out of it, citing all the reasons it wasn't possible, all the people and circumstances that would prevent him from achieving it.

Reasonable Aspiration

The sweet spot in the middle for a leader—that place I call being farsighted—is where you are not visioning too big or too small: you're creating a vision that's a reasonable aspiration for you and your business. (Before I offer a technique for creating this kind of reasonable aspiration, I'll mention that I've written another book explaining this process in much greater detail. It's called *Being Strategic*, and you might find it useful in developing the leader qualities we're discussing, especially farsightedness and wisdom. What I'm about to share with you is a kind of CliffsNotes version of some of the learning in that book.)

The starting point for reasonable aspiration is to get clear about your current reality because it's hard to envision a possible future that's good for the business without knowing where the business is now. One mental skill that comes in handy as you're trying to do that is what I call "becoming a fair witness." I borrowed this from *Stranger in a Strange Land* by Robert Heinlein. In the book, Heinlein invents a profession called Fair Witness. At one point, a character in the book named Jubal is demonstrating what a Fair Witness does: Jubal points to a distant house and asks the Fair Witness what color it is. She replies, "It appears to be painted white on this side": a Fair Witness is trained to simply observe and report, without inference or extrapolation.

If you want to develop your leadership quality of farsightedness, first work on becoming a fair witness about your current situation. I've often seen Bonnie Hammer demonstrate this first part of farsightedness. In meetings, when people on her team sometimes overstate the importance of some element of the current situation or, more often, try to dismiss or gloss over a difficulty or challenge, she brings the conversation back to fair witnessing by encouraging the group to explore the facts of their situation as accurately as possible before setting goals for the future.

Once you feel that you're clear about the current reality of your business or your department, you can begin to build a vision for the future.

Envisioning a Possible Future
Here's the approach I recommend:

1. Pick a time frame for success.
2. Imagine yourself in that future.
3. Describe what success looks and feels like.
4. Select the key elements.

Now we'll go into this in detail:

1. *Pick a time frame for success.* Begin by deciding on a reasonable time frame for success. You can use this approach for envisioning successes of any size, from making a compelling presentation to establishing a solid start-up, from building a high-functioning team to building a profitable international company. It's important that you pick a time frame that's realistic given the size of the challenge before you: a few weeks to a successful presentation; a year for a high-functioning team; a few years for a thriving start-up.

2. *Imagine yourself in that future.* This is where you overcome your mind's resistance to letting go of current limitations. To do so, you need to give your mind free rein to create a three-dimensional piece of a possible future. Put yourself into a mental time machine. Imagine emerging from your time machine into the same room and the same chair you're in now, but it's the date you've chosen above: you've returned to this room, this chair, to celebrate the fact that you've created your hoped-for future. It helps if you support your envisioning with a statement. For instance, "It's now January 19, 20xx, and I'm reflecting on my success creating the future I want." Once you feel comfortably settled (in your imagination) in this future date, go on to the next step.

3. *Describe what success looks and feels like.* As you mentally look around this new world at the end of your time travels, what do you see? Think about key events, feelings, circumstances, and outcomes that indicate to you that you've successfully created the future you want. If you're envisioning the successful future of your team, you might want to focus on some of the following: the results you're getting; what it's like to work on the team—both how it feels and how things actually happen; what other people see (and say) when they look at or interact with you and your team; and how you're fulfilling your role as the leader. (Some people like to simply visualize these things, while others find it helpful to jot down their thoughts.)

4. *Select the key elements.* When you feel that you have a fairly robust picture of this future you want, select and write down the key

elements—those parts of the future that are key to your vision of success. I suggest you write down the handful of things you feel are the most critical indicators of the future you want to create. You can do this in a couple of ways. Some people simply review their thinking and write down the elements that are most important to them. For instance, you might have imagined there would be a better coffee machine in the break room, but that's not as important to you as your vision of your team's consistently sharing important information with each other. Some people like to look for patterns and group the elements they've envisioned into key categories.

Try It: Envisioning a Possible Future

Now I'm going to give you a chance to try this out. You may remember I said I was going to offer you ways to build these leadership qualities. Here's the first one. If you rated yourself low in this first element of farsightedness—seeing a possible future that's good for the business—I suggest you work through this activity. (Even if you've rated yourself high in this behavior, you still might find this activity useful and interesting.)

I suggest you grab a notebook for doing the activities throughout this book; call it your *Leading* notebook. Most people (me included) hesitate to write in books, and if you're reading this on an e-reader, it might not be possible. So throughout the book, when I encourage you to write something down, go to your notebook.

Define the Challenge

First, I suggest you do what I call defining the challenge: clarify the area for which you want to envision success. It's useful to put this in the form of a question: "How can we . . . ?" or "How can I . . . ?" For instance, your challenge question might be: "How can we create a truly high-performance team?" or "How can I build my new business to be thriving and profitable?" Write a challenge question in your notebook that resonates for you and describes a challenge you want to address.

Now spend some time reflecting on your current state relative to this challenge. Write in your notebook the main things in your current situation that could support you in addressing your challenge (strengths, skills, or resources) and the things that could make it more difficult (deficiencies or roadblocks). Work to be as fair a witness as possible.

Here's an example. Let's say your challenge question is, "How can we get better at responding to our customers' needs?" When you look at your current situation relative to that challenge with fair witness eyes here's what you might see:

Circumstances or Resources That Could Support Me
We have a great research team.
Customers are willing to give feedback.
My boss gets how important this is.
We take pride in serving our customers.

Circumstances or Deficits That Could Get in the Way
We think we know what customers want—but we may be wrong.
We're slow in changing our approach.
We don't have good systems for gathering and responding to external feedback.
The CEO may not be willing to invest in this.

Select a Time Frame
Once you've framed your challenge and have a relatively clear sense of your current situation relative to that challenge, pick a specific date in the future that will allow you to have made substantive progress toward addressing your challenge. But be sure it's not too far away to see clearly; anything more than a few years out is usually hard to envision accurately, especially when you're just learning to think in this way. Write your selected date in your notebook. Trust me, it makes it more real to write it down, which is important for the next part of the exercise.

Imagine Yourself in That Future

You're now in the same room, same chair, same book, but it's the date in the future you've selected. Really let your mind get into the idea that you're now in that future date. You might want to reinforce this by saying aloud, in the present tense, a few things that you know will actually have happened on that date: "My son has finished middle school," or "My sister turned forty last year."

Describe What Success Looks and Feels Like

When you feel firmly grounded in this future date, think about how your challenge has been addressed. What's happening? How does it feel? How does it look to you and others? I suggest you jot down your thoughts in your notebook.

Select the Key Elements

Review what you've written, and capture the key aspects of your vision that are most important to you. Four or five is a good number of key elements—enough to capture your vision but not so many that it will become generic or difficult to remember or communicate. Write them in your notebook. You might find you've already focused on the key ideas from your brainstorm that best capture for you the important elements of your hoped-for future. Or if you're more visual, you might look at what you've written and find you can group your ideas into categories and then name the categories.

For example, you might have written a number of ideas focused on how you'll gather and use customer information in the future you've envisioned. When you look through those ideas, you notice they all relate to having a clear, simple process for gathering and reviewing the data regularly and then making development decisions based on what you see. You might summarize this first key element of your envisioned future by writing:

We have a dashboard of current customer needs and use it for decision making.

In other words, rather than, "We will create . . . ," write, "We've created . . . ." That will help you to see the future you want to create even more clearly.

There you have it: your first exercise in seeing a possible future that's good for your business. Like any other skill, it strengthens with use, and this particular skill is easy to play with. If you're interested in developing this aspect of farsightedness, you can apply this exercise to almost any situation, from envisioning a great vacation, to the resolution of a difficult interpersonal issue, to seeing how you'll achieve your yearly business goals.

#2 Articulate the Vision in a Compelling and Inclusive Way

As I listened to Bonnie speaking to the Universal Cable Productions team about the future they could create for themselves, I noticed three things: she spoke with *clarity and confidence*; she spoke in terms that the people listening *related to and found meaningful*; and she shared her vision from a *genuinely "we" rather than "I" perspective*, focusing on what she and they together could accomplish. These are the three elements that make a leader's expression of his or her vision both compelling and inclusive. Let's pull this apart, so you can learn how to share your vision in this way.

Speaking with Clarity and Confidence
The five behaviors of farsightedness build on each other. Once you can see a possible future that's good for the business, for example, it's much easier to express it clearly. The last step of the previous activity, selecting the key elements of your vision, is especially helpful in this regard. Once you've distilled your vision of a possible future into a handful of key elements, it's much easier to speak about it simply and clearly.

Repetition can also bring clarity. I find that when I come to a new idea or way of seeing something, it can be a little foggy in my thinking. But once I've identified the key elements, thought through them a few times, and tried explaining my vision to a few people (I usually start with people I know will be patient and supportive, like my husband or my business partner), I find I get clearer and more focused in both my understanding and my expression of the idea.

Of course, repetition can also sometimes reinforce a lack of clarity. I've heard people say untrue or unclear things over and over again, and they're still not true or clear. If you're repeating something to convince yourself or others that it's true, that won't make it true. The kind of repetition that leads to greater clarity arises out of curiosity. If you're repeating something because you want to test the idea and see if it's powerful, if it actually makes sense when looked at from various angles and from what reaction others will have to it, then repetition will probably make it clearer and clearer.

What About Confidence?

This kind of repetition helps build confidence as well. As farsighted leaders do this curiosity-based testing of their vision—as they talk about it, think about it, ask others to weigh in, and it still seems like a possibility—they gain confidence in its power and potential.

One leader I know who's especially good at this aspect of farsightedness is Josh Sapan, the president and CEO of AMC Networks. Over the years, I've watched Josh throw out ideas about possible futures to his team, using a "where we could go" and "who we could be" frame that most people find both compelling and inclusive. At first, he can be charmingly self-deprecating about the possibility he's presenting. And sometimes the ideas turn out to be unrealistic or not useful. Josh may then be the first to let them go. But often the ideas take shape and acquire heft and power in the interchange, and as that happens, I see Josh and the team gain ever greater confidence in the future they're envisioning. I notice that even people who may not have been engaged by the idea begin to feel the pull of the possibility: it becomes increasingly compelling to them as it's shaped in conversation. And this approach, of reflecting on and discussing an idea together, is by its very nature inclusive. Under Josh's stewardship, the AMC Networks brands have grown and prospered dramatically and continue to break new ground in the media landscape. I believe Josh's ability to envision new possibilities and then express them with increasing clarity and confidence is an important element of that success.

Try It: Getting Clear and Confident

Here's a guided activity to give you a way to try out these ideas about speaking with clarity and confidence.

Begin by reviewing the key elements of the possible future you envisioned earlier. Think about times you've gotten clearer and more confident about new ideas in the past. What approaches work well for you? Do you do best when you review them in your head? Write them down? Share them with others? Some combination of these? Write in your notebook ways you've tried that have worked for you and ways you haven't tried but you think might work for you.

Given your preferred clarifying approach, decide and write in your notebook the steps you'll take over the next few weeks to help you clarify and gain confidence in the vision you wrote down earlier. For example, you might write something like the following:

I'll rewrite my key elements in narrative form. Then I'll share them with my friend Alice, asking her to first listen and then let me know what's not clear or doesn't make sense to her. If talking to Alice makes me feel clearer and more confident, I'll take it to my team to see what they think.

Finally, read through what you've written in your notebook and add the dates by when you will have completed each of the steps. Giving yourself a time line makes it much more likely that you'll fulfill commitments you make to yourself.

Speaking in Terms That Engage the Audience

I once had the uncomfortable experience of being in the room while a CEO addressed a group of her junior employees in a way that was almost completely unintelligible to them. They were young people, mostly entry level and mostly just out of school, and this executive was talking about the need to build a better story about the company's future for the Wall Street analysts on the next quarterly market call. Her audience wanted to understand, and they wanted to be engaged—in fact, they felt honored that the president was spending this time with them—but as she droned on and on, I could see them starting to glaze over and get restless. She was talking *at* them rather than *to* them, indulging in a monologue about something that was important to her but not to them. By the end of their forty-five minutes together, she had completely lost them. She may have had a clear vision of the future, but she wasn't expressing it in a way that was compelling or inclusive for that group.

As you read through the fairy tale in Chapter Two, you may have noticed that the boy-leader's ability to focus on the greater good is an essential part of the story. He wants to succeed—but he wants to succeed by achieving a result that benefits others. Threaded through each of the six leader qualities, starting with this first quality of farsightedness, there's an element of selflessness. We look for leaders we believe will lead for the good of the group rather than for their own personal gain at the expense of the group.

When you speak about "where we could go" and "who we could be" in terms that connect with a particular audience, you are demonstrating your awareness of and care for that audience. When you as the leader frame your vision in this way, those you lead can see and feel that your vision includes and is meaningful for them.

Here are some practical ideas for speaking to those you lead in ways that engage them and resonate with them.

Start by Listening

In another book I wrote a few years ago, *Growing Great Employees*, I proposed that listening is the foundation of success for those who manage others, and I devoted the entire first chapter of that book to teaching my readers how to become better listeners.

I also believe that listening is the foundation of success for those who want to lead; being able to listen well is intrinsic to each of the six leader qualities. My work with good and great leaders over the past twenty years has shown me that it's possible to be truly farsighted, passionate, courageous, wise, generous, and trustworthy only if you listen deeply and consistently to those you lead. I'll be touching on the importance of listening at some point in every chapter of this book. Since this is the first place it has come up, I'll spend some time now explaining why it's important in this context. I've also put a fairly in-depth primer on how to become a more skillful listener at the end of the book, after the Epilogue, as a kind of bonus section, and I'll refer to this learning throughout the book.

If you're going to speak to people in ways that engage and resonate, you have to understand who those people are and what's important to them. Listening is the best and fastest way to find those things out.

When I was listening to the CEO who talked to her junior employees about the story she needed to tell on the quarterly call, it was clear to me that this woman hadn't made it her business to find out who these people were and how she could connect with their hopes and concerns about the organization and their success within it. If she had spent just a few minutes listening to find out about her audience and what was important to them, and then framed her speech based on that information, they would have left feeling excited and hopeful, glad to have her as their leader rather than confused and disconnected, questioning her leadership.

Fortunately listening is a learnable skill, although it's rarely taught. We've all heard we should "listen better," or "listen more," but those admonitions are almost never followed with insight about how to do it. This book's bonus section will support you in becoming more adept in this critical leadership skill. I invite you to read through it now or whenever you get to a point in the book where you start thinking, *I really need to become a better listener.* (If you're interested in more in-depth listening skill development, I invite you to read *Growing Great Employees.*)

Try It: Using Listening to Support Farsightedness

Refer back to the "possible future" you created earlier in this chapter. Think about someone you'd like to share it with, especially if it's someone who's key to the idea's success. Put this person's name in your notebook.

Below his or her name, write some curiosity-based listening questions you could ask this person before you share your idea, to find out how he or she might feel about this idea or any experience this person has had in the past with other ideas like it. For example, you might ask:

How do you think we're doing in terms of our response to customers?

How could we get a better sense of our customers' needs?

What do you think are some of the obstacles to being truly responsive to our customers?

Sometime in the next few days, strike up a conversation with this person. You might start by saying that you'd like to share an idea you have, but first you'd like to find out a little more about his or her feelings, ideas, or experience relative to the topic. Ask one of the questions you've jotted down in your notebook, and as the person begins to talk, try out all four listening skills: attending, inviting, curiosity-based questioning, and restating.

When you think you have some solid information about how the person might see an idea like yours and what might be important to him or her, share that idea, building on what you've heard.

After the conversation, consider the following questions:

- How did you share the idea differently than you might have before listening?
- How do you think using this approach may have changed the person's response?

Listening is key to both good management and good leadership, and I'll be suggesting various ways for you to use these skills throughout the book. I also encourage you to try them out in a variety of situations: at work, at home, with friends. Like any other skill, listening improves with use, and you may be surprised to note the impact your improved listening has on you and on others.

Speaking from a "We" Versus "I" Perspective

The first time I met Josh Sapan many years ago, he had stopped into a meeting that one of his direct reports was having with her team. They were talking about whether to create Web sites in support of their TV networks, a fairly new idea at the time. He listened for a while and then said, "You know, it seems important to think about this not from right now, but from where things are going to be in ten years. I think we'd regret not having done this, looking back." He was the boss's boss, but he entered into the conversation about the future from the point of view of "we're all in this together" rather than "I'm the leader, and what I say goes."

As I've worked with Josh and other good leaders over the years, I've seen that their inclusive approach of "we" is more than a superficial choice to use one set of words (*we, us, ours*) over another (*I, me, mine*); it arises from their view of the world. Josh, Bonnie, and other farsighted leaders genuinely look at the future they envision as something that will require the commitment and effort of their whole team to achieve, and so that's how they speak about it.

In other words, speaking from a *we* versus *I* perspective arises out of a belief that *we* are responsible for success, that *we* will work together to achieve the goals of the organization. People are wired to look for and accept leaders who believe that success will come when the group works together to reach it.

To create a "we"-centric belief system, start to notice your current beliefs and whether they serve you.

Try It: Establishing "We-Focused" Beliefs

Select an important business goal for which you're accountable—something your boss (or your board, if you're the CEO) is expecting you to accomplish. Think about this goal and how to achieve it. Being as honest as possible about your current state of mind, write down your beliefs about reaching this goal: who will be involved, how you'll interact with them, what you and they will do, and so forth.

Then reread what you've written in your notebook and reflect on the following questions:

- Who are you thinking of as being responsible for accomplishing this goal?
- How are you thinking of those around you relative to this goal? Supporters? Obstacles? Partners? Irrelevant?
- When you think about achieving this goal, what seems most difficult to you about it?
- Whose point of view about this goal are you taking into consideration?

Pick a part of your response that might get in the way of thinking and talking about the goal from a "we" perspective. For example, if in response to the question, "What seems most difficult to you about it?" your immediate thought was something like, "Others' resistance," or, "Having to get other people to do things," those beliefs will make it tougher to approach the goal from an inclusive perspective. Write down your most "non-we" response or belief in your notebook and consider how you might challenge that belief—for example, gather more information to decide whether it's true or ask others you respect for their opinion about the accuracy of your belief. Then write your ideas for challenging your "I" focused belief and note a date by when you'll do them.

If you do this and it changes one or more of your "I"-focused beliefs about this goal, I encourage you to then notice whether and how you speak differently about the goal to those around you.

#3 Model Your Vision

This aspect of farsightedness focuses on practicing what you preach. There's a wonderful story about Mahatma Gandhi that I often tell to demonstrate the power of this behavior. Although Gandhi was a key political leader in the struggle for Indian independence from Britain, he was also considered a spiritual leader, a great saint. Many people would come to Gandhi asking for blessings or guidance. One day, the story goes, a young mother came to Gandhi leading her little boy by the hand, and said, "Mahatma Ji, my son eats far too many sweets, and I'm concerned for his health. If you tell him to stop, he will do it out of respect for you." Gandhi nodded, looked thoughtful, and then asked the mother to return in two weeks. Puzzled, the young woman did as he asked.

Two weeks later, she returned and waited again to have the chance to speak to the master. When she came to the front of the line, she bowed respectfully to Gandhi and said, "Mahatma Ji, I came to you before and asked you to help my son understand he must not eat so many sweets. You asked me to return in two weeks, and so here we are." Gandhi smiled and said, "Ah, yes. I remember." He turned to the little boy and said gravely, "Son, your health is very precious, and eating too much sugar could hurt your body and your teeth. You must stop eating so many sweets. Will you do that?" The little boy ducked his head, awed, and replied, "Yes, Gandhi Ji."

The mother thanked Gandhi and then said, "Forgive me, Mahatma Ji, but why did you make us wait? I don't understand why you couldn't have said that same thing two weeks ago." Gandhi replied, "Two weeks ago, I was eating too much sugar myself. I had to stop before I could tell your son to do it."

Doing what you encourage others to do is powerful. When you model your vision, you can speak about the need to do so from a place of moral authority, as Gandhi did; your requests and suggestions are congruent with your own actions. Others can see that you hold yourself to the same standards you expect from them, that your vision is valuable and real for you. We want to know that our leaders' farsightedness is more than empty words; we want to be assured that they will be there with us as we move toward the future. Modeling your vision, living it day-to-day, communicates your commitment to that vision in a way nothing else can.

Vision as a Filter for Action

A few years ago, I was conducting a yearly planning meeting for Bonnie and her USA Networks team. USA had been the highest-rated cable network for a number of years, and its ratings were beginning to challenge those of the broadcast networks. Bonnie and her team started talking about the fact that in viewers' minds, the distinction between broadcast and cable was blurring. Viewers focused on their favorite shows more than the networks those shows were on, and more and more of their favorites were on cable.

I could tell that Bonnie wanted to give her team something more to aspire to. They were the top cable channel and had been for a while; she knew they now needed a new possible future to aspire toward. By the end of the meeting, they had agreed that their goal would be, "Become a top-three entertainment brand by breaking free of the limiting conventions of cable television," and they created strategies and tactics for achieving that goal.

Over the next year I watched Bonnie as she consistently used that vision of the future as a filter for action. In meetings, she would remind her team of the goal and ask them how and whether they were progressing toward it. When someone came up with a big idea for programming, or marketing, or PR, she would ask whether it would help them move toward the goal. She would point out and celebrate events and statements by others that showed they were moving in the direction they wanted to go. And she held herself accountable to the same standard, explaining why she believed the steps she supported would help them erase the line between cable and broadcast.

As the leader, keeping the vision in your mind as a yardstick by which to measure your actions, and then measuring what you and your team do against it, is a simple yet effective way to model your vision. Here's an approach to doing that.

Try It: Vision as Filter

Pick some aspect of a possible future for your team about which you feel strongly. It could be the goal you selected in the previous activity, the key elements of the vision you created earlier in the chapter, or some other important part of your team's hoped-for future. Write down the essence of it as simply as possible—a sentence or two is best—using words that resonate with you.

As an example, let's go back to the customer needs challenge we've been using. After reflecting on the four or five key elements you wrote down, you decide that the essence of your vision in this area is:

In two years, we'll know our customers' real needs, and we'll respond to them in ways that make them happy and drive our growth.

Now write down in your notebook three situations where you think it would be most useful and give the highest leverage for you to use your statement as a screen for your own and others' actions—for example, "our weekly staff meeting," "before committing to a new project," or "during budget planning."

Having made this commitment to yourself, I suggest you check back in a few months to see how you've done, and to think about ways you can model your vision even more consistently and effectively.

#4 See Past Obstacles

Seeing past obstacles is different from pretending they don't exist. Leaders who are farsighted are realistic (they have reasonable aspirations) and future oriented. So while they see the obstacles in the path ahead of them, they don't allow those obstacles to overwhelm them.

When obstacles arise, the true leader does his or her best to get clear about them and then figure out how to overcome them. I've watched leaders like Bonnie and Josh do two things in such situations. First, they make the effort not to underestimate or overestimate the magnitude of the obstacles. Then they engage others in working to address them. Just recently in a meeting, I watched as Josh did this: he kept bringing the conversation back until his team accepted and was ready to deal with a difficult aspect of the situation they were discussing. He wasn't trying to scare them, but he wasn't letting them off the hook.

Talking to Yourself About Obstacles

Most of us have a tendency to react to obstacles in one of two ways depending on our own particular wiring: we may tend to avoid looking at the obstacles or overbalance in the opposite direction and become completely paralyzed by them. The art here for a leader lies in taking the middle path: looking at obstacles simply as data, assessing them accurately, and deciding how to move beyond them to achieve your vision. That's what it means to see past the obstacles.

Learning to do this begins inside your own head, in managing how you're talking to yourself about the obstacles before you. Most people's mental monologue (self-talk) is a continual jumble of commentary. Some of it is pure reporting ("The industry is changing quickly") and some of it is highly interpretive and judgmental ("It's moving too fast. I'll never be able to figure this out!"). We tend not to make a distinction between the two types. We treat our interpretations and judgments as fact; we give all our self-talk equal legitimacy, and our objectivity about the obstacles facing us, or anything else, for that matter, goes out the window.

The extremely good news is that you can control your self-talk. You can bring your negative, inaccurate, or unhelpful mental comments to your conscious awareness and change them. This is extraordinarily helpful when contemplating the obstacles to your vision, a situation where many, if not most, of us tend to have unhelpful self-talk. In fact, managing your self-talk is, like listening, central to developing all your leader attributes. So, as for listening, I've written a brief primer on the skill of managing your self-talk, and put it in the bonus section at the back of this book, along with the listening section. You may want to read through it now, or at whatever other point in the book you get curious enough to investigate it. (I'll keep referencing the idea of self-talk, so you'll probably want to review it at some point.)

Try It: Managing Your Self-Talk

Now I invite you to try out the model to improve some unsupportive self-talk of your own:

1. Review the vision you created earlier. Think about the potential obstacles to achieving the vision, and record in your notebook any unhelpful self-talk that arises. As in the previous examples, it might be either negative and doubting or unrealistically positive—for example:

   We'll never make this happen. There's just too much organizational inertia.

2. Write the revised self-talk that you could use in thinking about the obstacles to your vision: self-talk that's believable and will support you in assessing the obstacles objectively and accurately—for instance:

   We actually don't yet know if this is possible. Let's think through the obstacles first. That will help us decide how to proceed.

3. Note a few ideas for "repeating"—that is, for making your rethought self-talk a new mental habit.

   Now you've created a self-talk statement that will help you to stay curious and open as you work to clarify the obstacles to your vision of the future or to any goal you may have. This more supportive self-talk will allow you to see the obstacles clearly and then to see past them as you continue to plan and move toward the hoped-for future you've envisioned with and for your team. (In addition to the bonus section at the back of this book, the topic of self-talk is also covered at greater length in my earlier book *Being Strategic*.)

#5 Invite Others to Participate in the Vision

Let's say you've done all the things already explored in this chapter, that is, all the behaviors that make up farsightedness: you've seen possible futures that are good for the business, articulated your vision in a compelling and inclusive way, modeled your vision, and seen past the obstacles.

This fifth behavior, where your farsightedness gets translated into forward movement for the group you're leading, is critical to being embraced as the farsighted leader. The first four behaviors get people to the point where they want to sign up. If you then limit their role to mere execution, you'll lose them. They may do what you tell them to, especially if you're their boss, but you probably will have forfeited the opportunity to engage their hearts and minds.

Remember that in the folktale, the boy-leader didn't just share his story with the little men; he welcomed them fully into his quest. They became his partners on the journey and ultimately offered him the key to saving the princess.

Fortunately, you've already learned key skills required to invite others into the process in a meaningful way. Being able to listen, establish "we-focused" beliefs, and manage your self-talk will give you a strong foundation for engaging others in the vision. Once you're using those skills, there's one more way, surprisingly simple, to ensure that you're inviting your team into the process.

Build In Collaboration

Every year, Josh takes the top twenty-five or so people in his organization away for a couple of days to think about the big issues facing them. The agenda includes some fun time and some time to enjoy each others' company, but the main goal is to step back from day-to-day work and focus on the future and how best to achieve it. It's a substantive conversation; important decisions often get made, and the group decides who will execute them. Then once a quarter, Josh brings the same group back together for the better part of a day to check in on the topics from the yearly meeting and address any new future-facing issues that have arisen. Josh most often is the person suggesting the focus for these meetings, but during the meeting, everyone is free to share opinions and ideas, take exception, or volunteer to move something forward.

I've seen this again and again over the years (Bonnie does her version of this same thing): good leaders, who have the full support of their teams, build in specific, practical opportunities to collaborate on crafting both the vision and the path to achieving it. I'm not talking about the more common kind of meeting, where the leader says, in effect, "This is what we're going to do, and here's who's going to do it," or even, "Tell me what you're doing, and I'll tell you whether I think it will lead us in the right direction." In contrast, the meetings I'm recommending are specifically designed around, "Let's talk about where we want to take this enterprise and how we're going to get there."

If, as a leader, you build this kind of meeting into your month-to-month and year-to-year operations and then use the skills outlined in this chapter at those meetings, it's highly likely that your team will rally around you as a truly farsighted leader and bring their best to working with you to achieve the future you've all envisioned.

Core Ideas

People want leaders who are farsighted. Before offering their full allegiance, they need to feel that the leader can see and articulate a future that's worth achieving and that he or she can guide them to it, past the obstacles that may arise.

Leaders who are *farsighted:*

- *See possible futures that are good for the enterprise.* They create reasonable aspirations by defining the challenges, getting clear about the current reality, and envisioning an attainable future.
- *Articulate the vision in a compelling and inclusive way.* They share "where *we* could go" and "who *we* could be" with clarity and

confidence, in terms that are meaningful to the group, with listening as the foundation.

- *Model their vision.* They practice what they preach: their actions align with the vision, and they remind and inspire others to act in ways that support the vision as well.

- *See past obstacles.* They assess the obstacles accurately by managing their self-talk, so they can craft practical ways to overcome them.

- *Invite others to participate in the vision.* They build in regular opportunities for the team to work together to clarify and then achieve a future to which everyone is committed.

FOUR

Passionate

The middle brother implored him, "Oh, little brother, let us go home and live in peace with our father. We've barely begun our journey, and look at the dreadful things that have happened already."

The younger brother replied, "You are welcome to go home. However, the princess is still held on her lonely mountaintop, and someone must save her, so I will continue."

The middle brother shook his head. "Little brother, think of all those smarter, braver, and stronger than you who have failed. Come back to our father's house with me."

"That's as may be," replied the younger son, "but I must do what I can do."

Finally, the middle brother pulled at his arm. "Be reasonable, little brother! Come back to the fireside; you are being foolish."

The lad smiled and repeated, "That's as may be, but still, I must do what I can do."

Nancy Tellem is listening intently. I'm telling her about my son's inspiring experiences with One Home Many Hopes, an organization in Kenya that rescues orphaned and abandoned girls and gives them the chance to lead lives of positive contribution. Nancy has a focused brightness, and she becomes very still as she listens. When I've finished speaking, she nods reflectively and then begins to tell me about her experience with Foundation Rwanda, a group that works with victims of genocide in

Rwanda, providing educational funding for the children born from rape, as well as medical and psychological services to their mothers, and also supports them in finding or creating income-generating activities. Nancy speaks quietly and with complete conviction; it is clear to me that she will do whatever is in her power to advance the cause of this organization and to enlist others in support of it.

I've seen her passion in how she approaches her profession as well. When she believes in something, she supports and works for it with true commitment, most often gaining others' support through the consistency and depth of that commitment. One very public example is from the late 1990s, when she was president of entertainment for CBS. She became convinced that *Expedition Robinson*, an incredibly successful Swedish show that had been considered too controversial for American TV, could become a huge hit here. It was about people trying to survive on an island and being asked to leave one by one (sound familiar?). She fought for it with a clear rationale and quiet determination, marshaling her team to overcome the financial and even psychological concerns. She gained the support she needed; *Survivor* first aired on CBS in 2000, and the rest is, as they say, history.

Nancy's passion has built her an equally passionate following. A few years ago, standing at a celebration with members of her team, listening to them speak of her with genuine affection, admiration, and respect, I realized that her passion, along with her other leadership qualities, had made her a true leader.

Passion in a leader is not just volume or manic energy. Many executives have pizzazz yet aren't accepted as leaders. Passion can be soft or loud, enthusiastic or quietly determined. It is not an obsessive focus on some idea or outcome to the exclusion of other alternatives. It is a pure, abiding commitment to something meaningful: a cause, a vision, or a set of principles. To commit to something means to believe in it fully and to continue to be guided by your belief in it, regardless of setbacks and adversity. People who work with a passionate leader don't wonder what she stands for or whether she will abandon her principles when the going gets rough.

However, passion is not synonymous with dogmatism or inflexibility. A truly passionate leader invites and encourages dialogue. She wants others to share in her passion, not simply tolerate or be railroaded by it. The passionate leader doesn't simply say, in effect, "This is true [or incredible, or necessary] and we must all do it." She says, "I think this is true [incredible, necessary]. If you think so too, how can we do it?" A passionate leader enlists people. She is able to speak about her passion in a way that's appealing, draws people in, and touches them with the power of his or her commitment.

Why do people want passion in a leader? Because we want to feel that he or she will stick with us. If we align ourselves behind a leader, we want that person to stay the course: we don't want him or her to get bored, or distracted, or careless, and wander away from the fray. A leader who has passion emanates strength and hope, a sense of being grounded in something important. That invites belief in both the goal and the leader and brings out our best efforts. Of course, this can be dangerous if the leader is farsighted and passionate but lacks wisdom or trustworthiness. History is littered with the unfortunate followers of such incomplete leaders. But passion in a leader, when balanced by the other leadership attributes, unleashes our own passion and inspires us to do important things well.

How to Be Passionate

In order to help you develop this quality in yourself, I'll approach as I did the first attribute of farsightedness—by taking it apart to look at the key behaviors that comprise it. When you unpack passion, here are the key behaviors of which it consists:

Leaders Who Are Passionate

1. Commit honestly
2. Make a clear case without being dogmatic

3. Invite real dialogue about their passion
4. Act in support of their passion
5. Remain committed despite adversity and setbacks

As in the previous chapter, I'd like you to self-assess on each of these behaviors. For each of the five indicators, note how well you think you do this. Use a scale of 1 to 3 to rate yourself in the behaviors, where 1 is, "I don't do this consistently; it's definitely a growth area"; 2 is, "This is a strength of mine; I do it consistently"; and 3 is, "I am unusually skilled and consistent in this area; it's a key strength." Do your best to be as objective and honest as possible. Reflect especially on how you believe others might assess you in these behaviors.

#1 Commit Honestly

Years ago, I was sitting in the back of a room while the chief operating officer of a client company was speaking about the need for cutbacks. He certainly sounded passionate: he spoke with apparent conviction and was making a great for-the-good-of-the-business case. He outlined how he and his team were making the same sacrifices required of everyone else. Then someone sitting just in front of me turned to the person next to him and whispered, "That is such bullshit. I know for a fact that he stuffed a bunch of out-of-scope budget requests for his own group into last year's numbers so he could look good this year. He knew the cutbacks were coming."

Whoa. At least three of us in that room immediately retracted our faith in him as a good leader and our willingness to do as he encouraged us to do.

This is one of the things that most people continuously and almost unconsciously scan for in their leaders: Is this person authentic in his or her commitments? We want to know that our leaders are committing to things because they believe in them personally, not out of some fake, superficial, or self-serving motivation. When dealing with leaders, we're especially wary of being cynically riled up to follow a course of action that the leader doesn't even believe in: it makes us feel deeply misled.

To Thine Own Self Be True

Another passionate leader of my acquaintance is Peter Liguori, until recently the COO of Discovery Networks. Peter believes passionately in the power of the creative process and feels strongly that creative businesses need to stay focused on the creative side as well as the business side, no matter how big or complex they get. He commits honestly, based on his authentic beliefs.

For example, Peter has established a creative council at Discovery, consisting of sixteen of Discovery's most engaged and productive creative executives around the world (admission to the council is through nomination and selection). He believes passionately in the potential of this council to feed Discovery's creative energy and to have a positive impact on the whole organization. It's been fascinating to facilitate this group's meetings and watch Peter's commitment to the council keep it moving forward, even though everyone on the council (Peter included) has a demanding job. Council members are enthusiastic participants both during the meetings and in assignments outside the meetings, and they are clearly inspired by Peter's honest commitment to them and to the process.

When the leader commits honestly, based on his or her authentic beliefs about what's important, people tend to feel it and be drawn into new levels of engagement. If the endeavor is also personally important to them, the leader's commitment resonates on an even deeper level for them, and it inspires them to commit deeply and honestly based on their own passion.

Try It: Committing to What You Believe

Here's a chance to reflect on your own behavior, and stretch your muscles in this area:

Think about something to which you feel deeply committed out of an authentic belief in its importance. It could be personal—your

---

marriage, being a good parent—or it could be professional—helping the people on your team grow and succeed, making sure a valuable product or service gets to market. Write it in your notebook.

As you think about this endeavor to which you're committed, answer the following questions (there are no right answers; the purpose of this is to give you a chance to start reflecting consciously on the nature of commitment based on belief):

- How much attention do you put toward fulfilling this commitment?
- If someone asked why this endeavor is so important to you, how would you respond?
- What do you do to let others know how important this is to you?
- What feelings do you have when you think about this endeavor?
- What are you willing to sacrifice to make sure this endeavor succeeds?

Now review the vision you created in the previous chapter and ask yourself these same five questions. If you find you're answering the questions very differently, what would you need to change about the vision in order for it to generate those same feelings of deep commitment in you?

#2 Make a Clear Case Without Being Dogmatic

A number of years ago, I was facilitating a meeting where Nancy Tellem was encouraging a group of executives at CBS to consider going in a different direction with one aspect of their programming. She spoke clearly and simply, and it was obvious that she felt strongly about her proposal. But there was no kick—no sense, that is, that if others disagreed, she would view their thinking as flawed, no implication that hers was the only smart choice. However, when another very senior person then presented a different point of view, there was definitely a kick: the other person all but said, "That's a dumb idea, and anyone who agrees with it is dumb."

Truly passionate leaders are, in an important way, dispassionate: they can tell you very clearly why they believe deeply in something without making you feel like an idiot for not understanding or agreeing. Their commitment to a vision or a cause never draws its power from dismissing or belittling other points of view.

The Downside of Dogma

You can work on the clarity side of the passion equation by using the ideas and techniques discussed in Chapter Three for sharing your vision with clarity and confidence. But what about the "nondogmatic" part?

I've used the word *dogmatic* intentionally here. The dictionary defines it as "characterized by an authoritative, arrogant assertion of unproved and unprovable principles" and "given to the expression of opinions very strongly or positively, as if they were facts." Dogmatism, in other words, is a tool that poor leaders use to try to shoehorn their passions into their followers. They do this first by implying, or stating outright, that any opposing point of view is wrong, as in the example I gave. Politicians in the United States often do this by claiming that those who don't agree with them are "un-American." I've sometimes seen this sink to the level of witch-hunting in organizations: people getting fired for simply disagreeing with the leader, meetings where requests for comments are greeted by dead silence because people are afraid to speak up.

Dogmatism also shows up when leaders state their point of view as an incontrovertible truth rather than as a considered opinion. Here's an example. Read the following statements, and note how each one hits you:

"It's obvious the only solution to our problems is to get better at building our client base."
"We've got a great product, but we're overrelying on our existing customers for growth. I think we need to find a better, more systemic way to build our client base."

I suspect when you read the first statement, there was something in you that went, *Oh, yeah? Says you!* We don't like being told what's so without anything to back it up. On reading the second one, you may have thought something like, *That sounds reasonable. I'd like to hear more.*

I've noticed that young leaders especially can fall into the trap of feeling that they need to be dogmatic in order to be seen as powerful. In my experience, the opposite is true. At one point when Peter Liguori and I were talking about a summit we were planning for the Discovery Creative Council, he suggested they spend some time focusing on how to improve the organization's creative process. I disagreed initially; I thought the council should focus more specifically on generating creative ideas. Peter listened carefully to my disagreement, then offered a clear and impassioned rationale for his point of view: he felt strongly that the council members, as creative executives, were most affected by any problems with the creative process, and would have great insights into how to solve them. He also explained that he was concerned that having the council come up with great creative ideas, and then putting them into a less-than-great organizational process, would be frustrating and counterproductive. He made the case that focusing on the creative process was the more foundational and strategic place to begin.

Peter never told me my point of view was wrong, and he never implied his point of view was the only way to see the situation. But he made his case so clearly and with such honest passion that I was sold. We ended up having a meeting focused on the creative process that has had a positive ripple effect throughout the organization.

Try It: Clarity Without Dogma

I invite you to check yourself for clarity and dogma. It's hard to do this alone; many of us, in fact, have a pretty big blind spot in this area. That is, we think we're clearer (if we have a tendency toward lack of clarity) or less dogmatic (if we have a tendency toward dogmatism) than we actually are.

Here's how to do it:

1. Pick a friend, colleague, or family member whose opinion you trust and who will be honest with you. Ask this person for fifteen minutes of his or her time to help you grow as a leader.
2. Select a topic that you feel strongly about—one that you've spoken passionately about in the past. Sit down with the person and let him or her know you'll be talking about something you find important.
   - Ask this person to listen for two things: how easy or difficult is it to understand the point you're making and how open you seem to considering an alternative point of view.
   - Talk about the topic as you normally would.
3. When you're done, ask your friend for feedback on the two points above. If this person had a hard time understanding your point, ask what you could have done to be clearer. If he or she saw you as being closed to other points of view, ask what you could have done differently to communicate your openness. You can use your notebook to make notes about the feedback and how you intend to address it.

This exercise will generally help sensitize you to your own tendencies going forward. Next time you speak on a topic about which you feel passionate, you're likely to listen more closely to yourself and to be clearer and less dogmatic.

#3 Invite Real Dialogue About Their Passion

Even if you don't speak dogmatically about your passion, you might still come across as dogmatic if you fail to engage others in genuine conversation about it. If Peter had said exactly the same things I noted above in our conversation but hadn't allowed me to share my point of view or hadn't listened to me when I did, the conversation would have felt completely different. I believe I would have been much less likely to have changed my mind and come around to his way of thinking.

The skills of listening are, as you might suspect, your most powerful tool in this regard. If you haven't yet done so, you may want to read the bonus section on listening at the end of the book now.

As I have noted, each of the six leader attributes rests on a foundation of listening. In some ways, this is especially true of passion, because passion on a topic can easily drift into obsession, dogmatism, or close-mindedness. The sweet spot of passion is almost oxymoronic: it consists of powerfully stated, deeply held opinions, combined with an openness to alternatives and to integrating what you hear into your existing point of view.

Being especially careful to listen deeply in areas where you feel most passionate is a simple and effective way to find that sweet spot. Here's one specific thing to do in order to take advantage of the power of listening: whenever you share one of your strongly held beliefs with someone else, remind yourself to pause and specifically invite his or her response. Ask, "What do you think about this?" or, "I'd love to hear your point of view on this too."

And when they respond, *and especially if they disagree*, remind yourself to get curious and really listen: attend, invite, question, and restate. You may hear something that truly informs or changes your point of view. And even if you don't, the people you're speaking with are likely to be much more open to your point of view if you demonstrate your openness to theirs.

#4 Act in Support of Their Passion

Modern media may have many unfortunate characteristics—bias, sensationalism, superficiality—but there's one way in which the media are very useful: negative stories about leaders are quite often a good indicator of the things we find most unacceptable in our leaders. I've noticed that leaders who lack the qualities I'm discussing here and demonstrate that publicly are quite often pilloried in the press. And pointing out the disconnects in this area—leaders who don't act in support of their passion—is a particular favorite of the media.

For example, think of the various religious leaders who have been revealed to indulge in the sexual behaviors against which they rail most loudly from the pulpit; the business leaders who turn out to have a marked preference for products other than those they manufacture and tout; politicians who clearly don't apply to themselves the laws they espouse for others. These disparities between action and passion are recounted (and re-recounted) in the press; we seem to find them especially worthy of censure.

We don't like to be deceived by our leaders; it seems like a personal betrayal. We feel as though the person has willfully and cynically taken advantage of our belief in a cause, a principle, an enterprise, or in him or her to make us do things that he or she isn't holding himself or herself accountable for doing. It makes us question the wisdom of following the leader. We ask, "If he can so easily turn away from his principles, how else will he leave us in the lurch?" and we might even question our own hopes and beliefs: "If he doesn't really think our products are better than the competition's, maybe they aren't."

One common way I see this disconnect is as espoused passion versus action: leaders who invite a behavior and then punish people for demonstrating it. In fact, recently I had a rather pointed conversation with a leader I coach about just this thing. In a staff meeting, he had passionately bemoaned the fact the his team wasn't, as he put it, "stepping up to the plate with new ideas." And when someone finally got up the courage to do so, this leader immediately shot the idea down as untenable and simplistic.

If you aspire to be a true leader to others, it's especially important to be a fair witness about whether you're acting in accordance with your passion. It's all too easy to make excuses about why you "had" to behave in ways that weren't aligned with your passion: the religious leader who was "overcome by the devil" (evidently repeatedly); the politician whose "situation is different from that of his constituents." Observe yourself objectively to see whether you're living your passion. If you aren't, either change your behavior or stop telling others you're committed to something you're not.

Try It: Walking Your Talk

Here's a chance to use your fair witness skills. (Remember that fair witnesses speak only from their direct experience; excuses, caveats, and extenuating circumstances have no place in their reporting.)

Think of something you're passionate about in business: a way you believe people should behave toward one another, a point of view about how to get good results, or something else. In your notebook, summarize your belief—for example:

> I feel strongly that people should be judged on their fitness for a particular job based on their skills—both technical and interpersonal skills—and on their knowledge and experience, not on age, race, or gender.

In fair witness mode, review your behavior over the past few months, and write in your notebook how you have and haven't acted in accordance with your stated passion or belief. For example, you might note things like the following:

> I've acted in accordance with my passion by:
> Asking HR for a slate of diverse candidates when I have an open position.
> If I hesitate to promote someone, I reflect to make sure I'm focused on skills and capability rather than race, gender, or even a personal style that's different from mine.
> I haven't acted in accordance with my passion by:
> Not addressing this issue with a colleague I feel dismisses the possibility of putting women in senior engineering positions.

If there are ways in which you haven't acted on your passion, what can you do differently going forward? Write down your intentions, and make sure they are reasonable aspirations—changes in behavior you are actually willing and able to make:

#5 Remain Committed Despite Adversity and Setbacks

This is the bottom line for passion. When Nancy and I were talking about Foundation Rwanda, she mentioned that she had agreed with the organization's leaders to help them create a fundraiser at the Paley Center in Los Angeles, where she was a member of the board. A few weeks before the event, one of the organizers reached out to tell her that not very many people had signed up and they were worried about what would happen. Nancy could have simply commiserated, made encouraging noises, and gone about her business, but she's truly passionate about this cause. She decided to put herself and her reputation on the line: she sent out a message to her entire e-mail list, noting how strongly she felt about Foundation Rwanda's work and asking people to come and support them.

Hundreds of people showed up for the event—it was an overflow crowd—and tens of thousands of dollars were raised for the organization. It demonstrated to me both the power of a single passionate person to have a positive impact on the world and the power of sustaining a commitment in the face of adversity.

It's in situations like this that people most look to see whether their leaders are true leaders and deserve to be followed. It's relatively easy to stay committed to one's ideals when no one is challenging them and when everything's going according to plan. But when your principles are questioned or your passion is dismissed, especially by those in positions of greater power than you, that's when your followers will look to see how you react.

Look back at the exercise you completed on acting in support of your passion. Now review the situations where you may *not* have acted in accordance with your passion. What kinds of obstacles or setbacks seem to cause you to waffle or waver? Pressure from your boss? Worrying about others' reactions? Something being harder, more complicated, or time-consuming than you thought it might be?

I encourage you to create a self-talk sentence in your notebook to support you in staying true to your convictions when the going gets tough. (If you haven't already read the section on self-talk, it's in the bonus section at the back of the book.) It might be something like, "If I really believe in this, now's the time to truly demonstrate that." Or, "I can expect others to follow my lead only if I show that I can stay the course." It needs to be something that's both believable and motivating to you.

Core Ideas

People want leaders who are passionate. Hearing and seeing the leader's deep commitment to the success of the enterprise or to a set of principles or values around how to achieve that success inspires their own passion and assures them that the leader won't abandon them when the going gets rough.

Leaders who are *passionate*:

- *Commit honestly.* They genuinely believe in what they espouse. People are touched and engaged by the genuineness of their passion.

- *Make a clear case without being dogmatic.* They convey the power of their belief without dismissing or belittling others' points of view.

- *Invite real dialogue about their passion.* Their passion is balanced with openness: they want to hear and integrate others' points of view.

- *Act in support of their passion.* They walk their talk: their day-to-day behaviors support their beliefs.

- *Stay committed despite adversity and setbacks.* Their commitment isn't flimsy. When difficulties arise, they hold to their principles and find a way forward.

FIVE

Courageous

"We have conferred," said the leader of the little men. "I can get you to the top of the mountain. But it will be frightening."

The lad swallowed, his throat dry. "Tell me," he said.

"You've seen our dart blowers," the leader went on, gesturing at his weapon, "but you've not seen us use them. They have a strong magic."

He pulled a small bag from his tunic and hefted it in one hand. "We have a dust that can shrink you small enough to fit into my blower. And I can blow you on a breath of magic to the top of the mountain, where you will land softly and regain your normal size."

The boy sat silently thinking. He had always been smaller than his brothers, smaller than the other boys in the village. And the idea of being even smaller, smaller than an almond, was truly terrifying to him. What if he didn't return to normal? What if he didn't land softly, and was crushed on the mountaintop? What if . . . ?

But then he took a deep breath: "I will do it."

John McDermott has no idea how courageous he is. He is an extraordinarily personable and approachable leader, the head of global sales and marketing for Rockwell Automation, and most of the time he uses his relationship and influencing skills to get people working together and moving in the right direction. It's his preferred approach to leadership, and it works well for him. This management style is particularly appropriate because his team is spread out around the world and consists primarily of very senior salespeople who are used to running their own show. John is most often thousands of miles away, at Rockwell's headquarters in Milwaukee. The salespeople are a strong-minded, autonomous bunch, and they appreciate and respond well to John's collaborative approach and easy-going manner.

But when the situation requires it, I've also seen John make tough decisions with limited information—decisions that require him to do things that are personally uncomfortable for him. Behaving in these ways is core to our definition of courage.

For instance, a number of years ago, John had a very difficult situation on his hands. One of his direct reports was getting good results but was exceedingly difficult to work with and tough to manage; she often made decisions that she thought were appropriate, but in fact they weren't best for her peers or the company overall. Even more problematic, she was dismissive of John's direction. Because she wasn't part of the core sales organization, she told others that John didn't understand her part of the business.

Finally John decided to sit down with this executive and let her know that she needed to change her behavior in order to keep her job. Given their history and this person's personality, John knew she was likely to be either extremely defensive or try to avoid the conversation entirely, and that once she realized that John was committed to following through, she might very well decide to leave the organization. I watched John put everything in place to have this conversation as skillfully and professionally as possible, and to make plans for next steps if the conversation didn't have a positive outcome.

The conversation was, as you can imagine, no fun. But John made his position completely clear; he was respectful but firm. The executive didn't respond well and ended up leaving the organization within a few months. It was tough in the short term, but John had a good backup plan in place, and that part of the business is now working better than ever.

As I said, I don't believe John thinks of himself as being particularly courageous, but over the years we've worked together, I've seen him consistently push himself in this way to take tough stands on important issues, an approach that's personally uncomfortable for him.

More Than Physical Courage

We typically think of courage in the physical sense: a soldier storming a bunker with bullets whizzing above or a firefighter pulling a child from a burning building. This particular sort of courage is rarely needed in the workplace, but it offers clues about the essential nature of the quality. A firefighter who goes into harm's way to save a child, for example, has made a difficult choice quickly in the face of incomplete data: there is no way of knowing exactly how dangerous this task will be. The firefighter's choice puts him or her at risk, yet he or she takes this risk to benefit another person, acting in spite of his or her own fear and hesitation. This third point is particularly important. We tend to think of courage as a state of fearlessness, but true courage actually means acting on our beliefs and decisions in spite of our fears.

In the workplace, being courageous often means doing things that we don't want to do: we're not particularly skilled at them, or they're emotionally uncomfortable for us, or we've had unpleasant experiences doing these things in the past. And these fears or hesitations are very individual. For John, the situation was particularly difficult because he is by nature a supportive and positive person, and that's how he prefers to lead. For another leader, someone to whom that kind of get-tough-and-lay-down-the-law conversation comes more naturally, *not* responding that way in a particular situation might require courage. For that leader, the courageous thing might be to take more time to decide or be *more* supportive and flexible.

In other words, the truly courageous leader is personally courageous. I've been reading George R. R. Martin's Game of Thrones series lately (great examples of good and poor leadership, by the way); one of the heroes states that if a difficult thing needs to be done—someone must be beheaded, or a war must be fought—the true king does it himself rather than making his minions do it. Here in the twenty-first century, that translates into taking personal responsibility for difficult actions. For example, when the courageous leader has a tough message to deliver, she does so directly and not through others. She also has the courage to state clearly that it's her position or belief rather than simply hiding behind the mantle of her position.

However, the courageous leader also has the courage to change her mind in response to new information and take full responsibility for both the initial position and the new one. She admits mistakes and apologizes, even if it's uncomfortable or feels risky.

Deciding, When You Must

Courage in a leader also often entails acting on limited data. For instance, a CEO may face a choice about whether to invest in a new, expensive technology that involves acquiring an uncomfortable level of debt, but that also seems to have a strong potential for supporting the long-term growth of the company by making core processes much more scalable. The leader's team may be divided as to how to proceed; they feel it's risky, but they also see the potential upside. And they know the clock is ticking: the longer they wait to make the decision, the more likely it is that any competitive benefits from having the new technology in place will evaporate. So they look to the leader. If he has courage, he will make the best decision of which he is capable at the moment, regardless of incomplete data, personal risk, and his own fear, and commit to it fully. If he lacks courage, he'll either refuse to decide (which with time-sensitive issues is a decision in and of itself) or decide provisionally, without full commitment. This lack of commitment shows up if the decision has a bad outcome, at which point the uncourageous leader is likely to assert that he didn't actually make the decision ("I never said that") or blame someone else for the outcome ("If they'd just executed on it the way I told them to . . .").

Linda Yaccarino, president of cable entertainment and digital ad sales for NBCUniversal, is particularly good at making bold decisions in situations where information is scarce. When I first met Linda, she was heading up advertising sales for Turner Entertainment, where she and her group pioneered the use of tailored advertising, that is, working with clients to develop ads that aligned specifically with the content of the shows during which they appeared (for example, an ad showing a hand sanitizer being used at a school in a show set in a high school). When Linda first encouraged Turner to invest in creating the capability to offer this option to advertisers, there were scant data at best to show that such an investment would pay off. But based on the information she did have, Linda believed it would be a huge incentive to her advertising clients and that it was important to be ahead of others in her industry in making this opportunity available to them.

Turner supported her in this effort (she's also passionate, so I'm sure she made a great case for it), and her decision to move in this somewhat risky direction has paid off handsomely, in terms of both ad sales revenues and cementing relationships with important clients. But she had no guarantee at the time that this would be successful; it required leadership courage to commit to this direction and stay committed to it until it had a chance to bear fruit.

Why This Is Important to Us

Courage in a leader is a blend of toughness, decisiveness, willingness to move past one's own limitations, humility, and resilience. It involves making difficult business and personal decisions, overcoming fear and risk to act on those decisions, and responding to the outcomes of those decisions in a responsible way. People need courageous leaders in order to know that someone will make the tough calls and take responsibility for them. They need to know, to paraphrase Harry Truman, that the buck really does stop here.

When people observe their leader behaving courageously over time, they are much more willing to follow him or her into new territory; Linda's group, for example, was very much aligned behind her on this new approach. And when the courageous leader encounters obstacles as a result of his or her courage, people are also much more likely to demonstrate their support for the leader's courageous acts. John McDermott's people rallied around to fill in the gaps after his difficult executive left the organization.

When the leader lacks courage, people feel as though they need to protect themselves. They tend to withdraw their full commitment from the team and the enterprise and try to figure out how to mitigate the personal impact of their leader's lack of courage. In other words, if people don't believe that you'll be there for them when the going gets tough, they won't be there for you when you most need their effort and support.

How to Be Courageous

As in the previous chapters, I'll deconstruct this quality so you can see how to recognize and develop it in yourself or others.

Leaders Who Are Courageous

1. Make necessary, tough choices
2. Put themselves at risk for the good of the enterprise
3. Do things that are personally difficult
4. Take full responsibility for their actions
5. Admit and apologize for mistakes

Once again, I encourage you to self-assess in each of these behaviors. For each of the five indicators of courage, note how well you think you do it. Use a scale of 1 to 3 to rate yourself in the behaviors, where 1 is, "I don't do this consistently; it's definitely a growth area"; 2 is, "This is a strength of mine; I do it consistently"; and 3 is, "I am unusually skilled and consistent in this area; it's a key strength." Again, do your best to be as objective and honest as possible. Be a fair witness.

#1 Make Necessary, Tough Choices

This is probably the area where I've most often seen leaders fall short with regard to courage. One of the good news–bad news things about being a leader, especially a very senior leader, is that you're quite often free to follow your own path—even if it's not the right one. You can justify, to both yourself and to others, not taking necessary and difficult action, and no one will say to you nay, at least not to your face.

I suspect you've seen it in your own work life. How many times over the years have you said or heard someone else say of a leader, "Why doesn't he just decide already! It's been months!" or, "It's not going to get any easier the longer she waits. She's just delaying the inevitable."

Some leaders err in the opposite direction in this area: they'll make tough decisions but in a reactive, almost panicky way, without having considered the information that is available. Or, having made a decision, they change their minds, seemingly at random, making another decision with equal force.

The essence of this first part of courage is this: when a decision needs to be made, good leaders consider all the available information, make a decision, and follow through on it. They take full responsibility for the outcomes if it turns out to have been the wrong decision, a topic we turn to later in this chapter.

Failing to demonstrate this aspect of courage gives people the sense that you're a victim of circumstances—that you're not capable of doing what must be done in order to avoid disaster. It's unlikely they'll commit to you as a leader when they see you're not willing or able to make key decisions with limited information or in the face of opposition—especially since they know that those decisions are sometimes those most necessary to guide everyone to safety. When you are the leader, people are paying close attention to you. If your team or your organization is aware that you have been circling around an important decision for weeks or even months with no resolution, they will draw the conclusion that you don't have the courage to make the decision. Trust me; they *are* watching, and this *is* what they're thinking. (If there are legitimate reasons for the delay, share them. I'll explore this at length in Chapter Seven on generosity because this is about being generous with information.)

This is often a particularly difficult leadership quality to develop. It's easy to build a rationale in your head for not making tough decisions, especially when there's a dearth of hard information and the risk of failure is high.

One sad example is the recent failure of Borders books. At many points, the leadership of Borders must have faced the question of whether to change their core business model in the face of increasing competition from online book sellers, especially Amazon, and electronic readers. I can only imagine there must have been a great many meetings where leaders had the opportunity to make the difficult decision to change course. But they didn't.

Because I've observed this phenomenon so often and because it's so easy to rationalize your own lack of action (or overreaction), I've come to believe that it's critical to have a few deeply trusted advisers—external fair witnesses, if you will—to help you keep yourself honest when it comes to making tough decisions. This is especially important when your own tendency to justify your preferred default is exacerbated by your employees' unwillingness to tell you when you're off-base.

Try It: Support for Tough Choices

In addition to building a group of external fair witnesses, you can use your self-talk skills to help you see where you need their help.

In your notebook, write down a difficult decision you're wrestling with, or note an area in your personal or professional life where something isn't working well and you're not sure what to do—for example:

My teenage son is hanging out with a group of kids who aren't interested in school, and it's affecting his grades.

Notice your self-talk about this situation. Are you making excuses for your actions (or lack or actions)? Are you trying to convince yourself about something regarding this situation? Are you building rationales regarding why something is or isn't true? Note the essence of any "justifying" self-talk in your notebook, beneath your description of the situation.

He'll grow out of it.
Kids that age don't listen to their parents.

As fair witness advisers, pick people who know you and the situation well and who you believe will be able to offer objective, neutral counsel based on their observations. (You may want to write their names in your notebook.) It's important that these people support your ultimate success and are willing to be straight with you even if they feel it may be difficult for you to hear what they have to say.

Invite one or more members of your fair witness council to meet with you (perhaps over lunch or drinks—your treat, of course). Share the situation, and tell them what you've been saying to yourself. Ask them what they believe you should do, and why. Ask them to be completely direct and honest.

Based on your conversation with members of your council, revise your self-talk to support an accurate assessment of the situation and courageous action. Write your revised self-talk in your notebook—for instance:

It's essential that I find a way to talk to him about this.

or

I know if I don't address this, I'll regret it.

Once you've done all of this, then comes the hard part: you have to be open to your advisers' counsel, and act on it if it rings true to you. Even with wise and objective counsel, you're still the one who has to be courageous.

#2 Put Themselves at Risk for the Good of the Enterprise

I've often seen John McDermott do this. If he's convinced that a course of action is best for the organization—a change in structure or approach or a decision about people and their roles—he'll go to bat for it, even if his peers and his boss disagree. I've often seen him fight for an unpopular decision, even if doing so could damage his own career prospects.

Because John is such a relationship builder, he never does this in a belligerent or rigid way; he just quietly states his point of view and works to make sure others understand it. I've never seen him cave when it would be politically expedient to do so.

This aspect of courage sends a powerful signal to people about the quality of leadership. When others see that you're willing to do something that could damage you personally in order to support the success of the organization, they are hugely more likely to line up behind you. It's incredibly reassuring to see that your leader, who has more power over your career than anyone else in your organization and can fire you, puts the good of the organization before his or her own career success.

If, however, you observe that your leader is willing to sacrifice others or the good of the organization on the altar of his or her personal success, you'll be deeply unwilling to put your fate into that person's hands.

In fact, recently I was having a conversation with a client in a large media corporation. She said that what made her most uncomfortable about reporting to her boss was that she felt he would "throw her under the bus in a moment if he felt it would benefit his career." Yikes. Needless to say, my client is not going to go out of her way to support her boss's success.

Understand that I'm not talking about willfully blowing up your own career. Many years ago, I was facilitating a meeting when a hot-headed junior member of the team started to dress down the general manager of the company in front of the rest of the team. He told him that his approach to the crisis they were in was "ridiculous." I did my best to mediate but knew I was watching him commit career suicide. Afterward, another person said to me, "I wish I had that kind of courage." I responded, "That's not courage; that's foolhardiness. He could have made his point in a respectful way, one on one. *That* would have been courage."

Try It: Acting for the Greater Good

Your fair witnessing and self-talk skills will come in particularly handy here. You'll use an experience you've had as a case study and a model for moving forward.

Think of a situation in the past year when you failed to say or do what was best for the organization because you were worried about the potentially negative impact on you. It could be something as simple as not speaking up in a meeting to support an unpopular (but correct) point of view, or something as significant as letting someone go down a path you knew would be damaging because you thought you might damage your own reputation by trying to point that out. Feel free to jot down the particulars in your notebook. Then address these questions:

- If you could do it over, how would you behave more courageously in that situation today?
- If you think that behaving in that way might have damaged your career or relationships, what could you have done to mitigate that negative impact while still being courageous?

Now think about and summarize in your notebook a current situation where you have the same choice: to act for the greater good or to protect or boost your own standing. How can you act courageously in this circumstance while minimizing the personal negative impact as much as possible? For example:

I know we need to focus more consistently on improving the look and feel of our retail stores. Standing up for this is not going to make me popular with my store managers. They may even complain to my boss.

> If I give my boss a heads-up about what I intend and that he might hear complaints, that will help. I can also really focus on listening to my managers' objections and help them understand what's in it for all of us to improve in this area.

#3 Do Things That Are Personally Difficult

In folktales, there's always a place where the king-in-training has to do something designed to be particularly difficult for him personally. I love the scene in the first Indiana Jones movie where Harrison Ford says, "Why did it have to be snakes?" Of all the obstacles to be thrown in his way, snakes were clearly the most personally difficult for him.

This aspect of courage is really another version of putting yourself at risk for the good of the enterprise. Rather than risking your career, you're putting your comfort, your confidence, or your self-image at risk. And often that's even harder.

Avoiding Discomfort Can Backfire

We all want to be comfortable; it's how we're wired. But having the courage to get out of your own comfort zone when necessary is essential to your success as a leader. A few years ago when the Great Recession was in full swing, I was coaching a CEO who truly hated to give her organization bad news. She rationalized that it could make her look weak and that it would demoralize people. She also fooled herself into thinking that "just staying focused on the goal" (her phrase) without acknowledging current reality would somehow be motivating.

I had a long conversation with her about courage; I told her that I felt her folks were looking to her for the unvarnished truth: that cash flow and profitability were in a bad way. I even let her know that her people were aware that this kind of communication was hard for her and that seeing her take the uncomfortable step of sharing the tough financial picture with them would strengthen rather than diminish her in their eyes. Finally, I noted that if she told them the hard truth, so that they were operating with all the key information, they would be more capable of working with her to craft a way back to profitability.

Unfortunately, she wasn't willing or able to rise above her own discomfort to be honest with her employees about their situation. Three years later, the company is still struggling, and the board is questioning her leadership.

Try It: Do the Uncomfortable Thing

You can practice this capability in small ways on a day-to-day basis, creating a habit of courage that will serve you when larger issues come into play.

Write in your notebook four things that you regularly avoid doing that you know you ought to do—for example:

Calling Aunt Flo on her birthday
Letting my husband know I'd prefer he not listen to Garth
   Brooks when I'm in the car
Talking to my assistant about getting to work on time
Anything to do with snakes

Pick one, and do it. I don't want to hear any excuses: just go for it. (For the moment, think of me as your personal trainer of courage.) If you're the sort of person for whom writing supports action, make a written commitment about when and how you'll follow through.

That's it. If you practice doing little things you find scary, awkward, or embarrassing, then when you're called on as a leader to do a big thing that's scary, awkward, or embarrassing, it won't seem quite so daunting.

#4 Take Full Responsibility for Their Actions

I've never heard Linda Yaccarino blame another person when something she's done doesn't work. In fact, when I was first coaching her a number of years ago, I found it unusually easy to give her constructive feedback about her behavior as a leader; she would listen, ask questions if she needed more clarity, acknowledge the validity of the feedback ("Yep, I do that sometimes"), and then engage in figuring out how to change.

I've also seen leaders who do the exact opposite. When I (or others) give them feedback about something that's not working, they go into a flurry of denial and blame: it's someone else's fault; it's the way the organization is set up; their boss makes them act that way; and so on. Basically they are denying responsibility.

This failure of leadership is particularly upsetting to others. When people in an organization talk about a leader who behaves this way, it's invariably a cautionary tale: they want to protect others from being scapegoated by this uncourageous leader. Blaming others or denying responsibility is a dangerous misuse of power. As a leader, you have the option of pushing the negative consequences of your poor decisions onto other people by pretending that they're responsible for your decisions or that their execution of those decisions is at fault. And people recognize both the possibility and the danger of this. If you as a leader don't take full responsibility for your words and actions, people, especially those who work most closely with you, may obey you but they won't support you. They'll focus instead on making sure you can't blame them for your own failures. It becomes a "CYA" atmosphere, anathema to collaboration or innovation.

Many years ago, I worked for a wonderful man named Peter Block. Among the many useful and important things he taught me, one was a simple way to help people take responsibility for their actions. He noticed that when you're trying to diagnose a problem and you ask people what's causing the problem, they'll first focus on macroconditions, telling you all the contributing factors they see in the company, the industry, or the world. If you then ask, "What else?" most will focus a little closer to home, talking about how the people around them are creating the problem. But if you continue asking, "What else?" most people will stop there. They won't want to consider their own contribution to the problem. I learned from Peter that when you're in a tough situation, the most important question you can ask is, "What's my contribution to the problem?"

If you combine this question with your fair witness skills to help ensure that you're accurate in your assessment, you're much more likely to see what taking responsibility for your actions will require in a given situation. And—this may seem counterintuitive, but it's true—when you take responsibility for your actions and acknowledge your contribution to a problem, you will come across to others, especially those who work for you, as a much stronger leader.

Let's say that you've made a presentation to your boss and some other senior people that wasn't well received. They've told you to go back to the drawing board with your team and completely redo some key points.

It would be all too easy, in bringing the feedback to your team, to focus only on your boss's contribution to the problem: "She wasn't clear enough," or, "She didn't give us enough time to prepare," or, "She didn't give me all the information beforehand." And though your own folks might commiserate and stroke your ego a bit, how do you think this would make you look in their eyes? Not to put too fine a point on it: Whiny. Weak. Not leader-like.

Imagine if you instead came back and said, "The presentation didn't go as well as I would have liked. I may not have understood what the boss really wanted. But now I'm clear, and she's giving us another chance to get it right." I suspect they'd respect your honesty and forthrightness and come together to support you in improving the presentation.

Try It: Recognizing Your Contribution

Let's raise the bar here. I'm going to ask you to focus on a situation where you *really* felt justified in blaming someone else or some circumstance around you. If you can see and take responsibility for your own actions in a situation like that, you'll truly be stretching your courage muscles.

Think about a situation recently where something at work didn't go well, your self-talk has been entirely focused on others' responsibility, and you're convinced that it's all someone else's fault. Write down the particulars of the situation in your notebook (it's okay to vent a little). It might look something like this:

> I can't believe those people in marketing didn't tell me they were thinking about going in a whole different direction. We had agreed that the branding for the new model was going to be basically exactly the same as for the old model. Then when I finally see it, it's completely different!

Now ask, "What's my contribution to this problem?" Then notice your self-talk. It may be a flurry of self-justifications. Now become a fair witness: being as neutral and objective an observer of this situation as possible, ask yourself again, "What's my contribution to this problem?"

Write in your notebook how you'd explain your contribution to the problem if you were describing it as objectively as possible. In the situation above, that might look something like this:

> Even though they told me they felt strongly we should take advantage of the new model's features to do some rebranding, I wasn't open to it at all. I guess I didn't leave them much choice but to do it my way or go off on their own and get others' buy-in. Which is what they did.

Once you've written it down, review it to make sure it didn't veer off into blame or denial. If so, revise it. For example, saying "I guess my standards are just too high," is not an actual acknowledgment of your contribution; it's a backhanded way of saying, "It's not my problem if everyone else has low standards." If you're really being a fair witness, you might acknowledge your contribution by saying, "I didn't make a compelling case for doing it this way," or, "I didn't respect others' point of view about what was needed." Reread your statement and imagine how it would feel to say it to someone else.

You might be surprised; often it's a big relief to say, "I did something that wasn't a good or helpful thing; I played a part in this."

#5 Admit and Apologize for Mistakes

Admitting and apologizing for your mistakes is a specific and important form of taking responsibility. And not admitting one's mistakes or apologizing for them is another leadership failing that really upsets people and for which leaders regularly get pilloried in the press. I suspect Bill Clinton's weasely denials about sex and pot (among other things) and George W. Bush's evasiveness about his administration's mistakes regarding Hurricane Katrina and Iraq (among other things) will be remembered long after folks have forgotten most of the other particulars of their presidencies.

The Art of Apology

Since we've already looked at taking responsibility, let's focus here on how to apologize well. I'm a huge fan of good apologies; when they are genuine and warranted, they can resolve conflict, lower resistance, build respect, and disarm the toughest critic. I've often seen John McDermott apologize, and he does it very cleanly. "I'm sorry I wasn't clearer about what I expected from you in that situation," I once heard him say to an executive who works for him. "I want to make sure I'm being clear now." It was a perfect example: I'm sorry; here's what I did (with no caveats); here's how I'll fix it. And in that situation, I noticed that John received exactly the response that genuine apologies almost invariably get: apology accepted; frustration and ill feeling released; the other person ready to work with the leader to make it right.

Let's deconstruct good apologies, so you can make them yourself.

I'M SORRY "I'm sorry" or "I apologize" is the core of a genuine apology. It's the stake in the ground to communicate that you truly regret your behavior and wish you had acted differently. No apology is complete without this.

STAY IN THE FIRST PERSON Many, perhaps most, apologies run off the rails at this point when the apologizer shifts into the second person: for example, "I'm sorry; you didn't understand me," or, "I'm sorry you feel that way." Suddenly you're no longer apologizing for your actions; you're telling the other person that you regret his or her actions. A true apology sounds like, "I'm sorry I . . ." or "I'm sorry we . . ." (for instance, if you're apologizing to a customer on behalf of your company). In fact, here's a customer service example to illustrate this. Imagine you're having a problem getting credit for an item you've returned; you've been through a couple of people on the phone and finally asked for the manager. You've explained your situation, and the manager says either, *"I'm sorry you don't feel we've handled this situation properly,"* or, *"I'm sorry we haven't handled this situation properly."* I imagine the first one would just make you mad ("Wait a minute, buddy. I don't just *feel* you've handled it badly! You did handle it badly!!"). The second one would calm you down and make you feel heard. It would probably also give you the impression that the manager was an honorable and even brave person. It's amazing the difference that a few words can make.

DON'T EQUIVOCATE   Once you've said what you regret about your actions or words, don't water it down with excuses. That can blow the whole thing. The manager of my former apartment building once said to me, "I'm sorry we haven't gotten back to you about your security deposit, but you have to understand we've got hundreds of tenants." I definitely did not feel apologized to; in fact, I felt he was telling me I was being inconsiderate to hold him accountable for keeping his agreement with me! And CEOs do this way too often when speaking to their organizations: "We regret that we haven't made the changes to the retirement plans we promised, but our fourth-quarter results have made that inadvisable." When you add a caveat, it's as if you're no longer taking responsibility. You're now saying, in effect, "I would be sorry, but there's really nothing I can do about it, so it's not actually my fault, so apology retracted." Just let the apology stand on its own: "I'm sorry we haven't gotten back to you about your security deposit." "We regret that we haven't made the changes to the retirement plan we promised."

SAY HOW YOU'LL FIX IT   This seals the deal. If you genuinely regret your words or actions, you'll commit to changing. This needs to be simple, feasible, and specific: "I'm sorry we haven't gotten back to you about your security deposit. We'll have it to you by this Friday." "We regret that we haven't made the changes to the retirement plan we promised. We'll have a modified plan to you by the end of this quarter, and we'll follow through in implementing it."

DO IT   I know some people who don't have a hard time apologizing but seem to have a hard time following through on their apologies. If you apologize and say you're going to behave differently and then don't, it's actually worse than not having apologized in the first place. When you don't follow through, people question not only your courage but also your trustworthiness.

Try It: A Genuine Apology

Here's a chance to try this out.

- What's a current mistake or bad behavior you need to apologize for? (Come on, everyone has something.)
- To whom do you need to make your apology?
- Imagine looking that person in the eye and making a fully effective apology: "I'm sorry I . . ." Don't add caveats or excuses. Then note how you'll fix it. Write it in your notebook. (Feel free to steal from the examples I gave earlier.)
- Review it to make sure you haven't somehow weakened it in any of the ways discussed.

   I strongly encourage you to make this apology sometime in the next couple of days. Notice how you feel before you do it, while you're doing it, and after you do it.

Being courageous is generally daunting in anticipation. But it feels great once you've done it—to you and to those you lead.

Core Ideas

People need to experience a leader's courage. When the leader is courageous, people feel able to take risks; the leader's demonstrated courage provides a safety net for them. If the leader isn't courageous, people will feel they have to protect themselves and will fragment into self-focus and even paranoia. Collaboration and innovation will suffer.

Leaders who are *courageous*:

- *Make necessary, tough choices.* When a decision needs to be made, they consider carefully (even if information is scarce), make the decision, and follow through.

- *Put themselves at risk for the good of the enterprise.* They act for the greater good, even when it may threaten their own success.

- *Do things that are personally difficult.* They do what's required, even if it's personally uncomfortable or frightening.

- *Take responsibility for their actions.* They own their decisions, words, and actions rather than denying or placing blame.

- *Admit mistakes and apologize.* When they're in the wrong, they say, "I'm sorry I . . . ," without caveats, and they say what they'll do to fix it.

SIX

Wise

As he entered the stables, the boy saw many fine horses along one side and beautiful cages filled with colorful birds along the other. With a shock, he recognized his brother's big roan horse partway down the aisle. At the same time, one of the birds flew wildly to the edge of its cage and began to beat its wings against the bars.

The youngest brother ran to the cage. "Is it you, brother?" he asked. The bird dipped its beak as if nodding. The boy reached out for the cage's latch, but stopped the moment before his hand touched the ornate metal, remembering the beast-man's words.

Instead, he pulled the faery's shining coin from his pocket and rubbed it. The faery appeared at once on a sweet-smelling wind. The boy explained the situation, and she touched the cages with her shining staff.

One of the people around the table has just shared her very impassioned point of view, and Kathy Dore is thinking. We're sitting in a meeting with her executive team and an outside consultancy Kathy has brought in to help with a major acquisition. At the time of this meeting, she is the president of the Broadcast Division of Canwest Media, which is in the process of acquiring the specialty channels ("cable channels" in the United States) of Alliance Atlantis.

It's a huge and complex undertaking, made more complex by the Canadian laws affecting these kinds of corporate mergers. The Canwest executive who has just spoken with such passion feels strongly that the senior people on the Alliance Atlantis side should be told as little as possible about the acquisition. She's worried that it will distract them and may cause the folks they most want to retain to make plans to leave the organization after the acquisition.

I suspect I know what Kathy is thinking (she's been a client and a friend for years, and I know her well), but I'm looking forward to hearing how she responds. When the executive is done speaking, Kathy acknowledges her point of view and summarizes the concerns she's expressed. Then she offers the opposite point of view, noting how sharing as much information as possible could ease the stress of transition, signal openness and transparency, and allow people to make their decisions about whether to stay or leave based on real information, not gossip. Then she opens the topic up to the group, asking them what they think. As people discuss the issue, Kathy listens carefully, asking a question here, nodding thoughtfully there. After about twenty minutes, the group coalesces around the idea of sharing more versus less information. Kathy turns to the original speaker and asks, "Where are you now?" The woman says, "I'm okay with this direction. I'm still a little worried, but I see the benefits too."

I had the pleasure of supporting Kathy as our client for over a decade; now I have the even greater pleasure of having her as my colleague. In 2008, after finishing her contract at Canwest, Kathy decided to join Proteus. Kathy demonstrates all of the leader attributes, but none so much as wisdom. I witnessed the power of her wisdom to build strong teams and create great results in the companies she led, and now I have the benefit of having that wisdom applied to our own business.

Balancing the First Three Attributes

The quality of wisdom balances the forward motion of farsightedness, passion, and courage. Wisdom is the ability to reflect and understand, grow from that understanding, and share the insight that arises out of that reflection and growth. It is the process of consciously learning from one's experience and offering that learning for the benefit of others and the enterprise. Wisdom requires time and thought, curiosity and objectivity, logic and intuition. It requires a clear moral compass unhindered by self-righteousness.

First and foremost, the wise leader is deeply curious. She wants to understand—to see how things are wired together, to trace the connections among objects, events, ideas, and people. She's impelled to understand the shape of a situation so that she can act properly, provide useful insight, and learn and improve. Therefore, the wise leader gives the time and focus required to think deeply about important issues and to ask for others' perspective, help, or counsel.

Wisdom also requires the pairing of curiosity with objectivity. Curiosity is the impulse to investigate, the movement toward, "I wonder why . . . ?" or, "How does that . . . ?" But in order to lead to wisdom, curiosity must be informed by the fair witness spirit. Think of it this way: curiosity makes you want to dig; objectivity allows you to assess whether you've unearthed gold or lead. Objectivity is the ability to look at all sides of a situation with openness and dispassion.

Once again, your listening and fair witness skills are key (I told you I'd keep coming back to them). Real listening is the tool you dig with; it's how you act on your curiosity. And fair witnessing is the process of consciously becoming objective about what you discover.

Although wisdom requires objectivity, it also requires the ability to make intuitive leaps and see larger patterns. This requires a mental skill I call "pulling back the camera," which I'll teach you later on in this chapter: the essence of it involves looking at a whole situation in order to see the potential impact of specific actions or facts. I've often seen Kathy do this. The situation at the beginning of the chapter is a good example of this: she saw and helped others see how acting in a particular way—sharing information with the folks in the company being acquired—would support a larger goal of establishing a culture of trust and collaboration after the acquisition.

Do the Right Thing

Finally, wisdom has a strong moral component. The wise leader thinks not only about what will be the most effective or productive thing to do, but also about whether it is the right thing to do in a moral sense. When I was coaching the president of an organization recently, she told me that at one point in her career, the CEO of the organization had come to her and said they thought she would do a better job as head of marketing than her boss who held that position; he offered to fire her boss and give her the job. She told me she thought about it long and hard: she really wanted the job, but her boss had been unfailingly supportive of and honest with her, a true advocate. She finally decided that for her, it wouldn't be the right thing to do: it didn't feel like the morally correct choice.

Morality is rather complex and subtle; for one person it means never breaking a law, and for the next it means consciously and publicly breaking laws that he or she feels are unjust. Morality isn't cut-and-dried in the personal realm either: one person might feel it's morally wrong to have sex before marriage; another might feel it's an essential part of being able to make a strong commitment to marriage.

The important thing as a leader is to consciously develop your own moral sense—your best and truest understanding of right and wrong—and then act in support of your own morality. In other words, to do your best to do the right thing.

How Does This Look?

Think of a situation where a company's growth has stalled and the leader must decide how to respond. A wise leader looks at all the relevant information in an objective and systemic way to try to understand the root causes of the problem. He thinks deeply about possible courses of action, considering not only their long-term effect on the business's results but on the employees, the customers, and the company's reputation as well.

He invites the advice and insight of those he trusts and respects. He reflects on his own experience of similar situations in the past. In sorting through all of this, he'll look for a course of action that makes sense to his intellect, his gut, and his heart; he'll strive to do right *and* do well. Perhaps even more important, having made the decision, the wise leader will reflect again on the outcomes of his chosen course so as to be able to make better choices in similar situations in the future. And if the course he chooses turns out not to have been the best, he would reflect, clear-eyed, on his own process and experience so as to be able to learn from his mistakes going forward.

Why We Look for Wisdom in Our Leaders

Wise leadership gives people the confidence that important decisions will be given the thought they deserve and that their work lives will not be dealt with lightly, frivolously, or disrespectfully. We want to know that if we put our fate, at least our professional fate, in the hands of a leader, he or she will treat that as a sacred trust. When leaders are wise, we see that they're considering our welfare and that they'll do their best to make sure that the enterprise succeeds in a way that supports the success of the greatest possible number of us, their followers. Wise leadership feels like the safest possible harbor, especially in times of great change.

How to Be Wise

You won't be surprised to see that I've deconstructed wisdom into five behaviors. (I actually didn't set out to do this, for those of you who might be wondering. Each of the leader attributes naturally fell into five discrete behaviors as we were developing and using them in our work with leaders over the years.) I think you'll find the behavioral indicators especially useful here, as wisdom can seem amorphous and ill defined, but in fact it is both definable and developable. Here's what we've discovered.

Leaders Who Are Wise

1. Are deeply curious; they listen
2. Assess situations objectively (fair witness)
3. Reflect on and learn from their experience
4. See patterns and share their insight with others
5. Act based on what they believe is morally right

I'll encourage you to take a little time here to reflect on your own current capability—what you actually do versus what you'd like to do. Then use a scale of 1 to 3 to rate yourself in the five behaviors, where 1 is, "I don't do this consistently; it's definitely a growth area"; 2 is, "This is a strength of mine; I do it consistently"; and 3 is, "I am unusually skilled and consistent in this area; it's a key strength."

Look at this self-assessment as an exercise in wisdom: do your best to be curious about your own current state, assess yourself objectively, and look for patterns in your own behavior as you complete this initial assessment.

#1 Are Deeply Curious; They Listen!

Deep understanding is the foundation of wisdom. In order to gain that understanding, you have to be curious, and you have to listen. As I said earlier, curiosity is the impulse to investigate, and listening is the tool you use to carry out that impulse.

Every truly effective leader I've met is curious and a good listener. Each of the leaders I've used as exemplars in the previous chapters consistently looks to find out more or understand more deeply; each one listens well and often. In fact, I don't believe it's possible to be a fully accepted leader without curiosity and listening.

I know that many people who are neither curious nor good listeners become highly placed and highly paid leaders. And I know some very powerful leaders who aren't curious and don't listen to their followers at all. But I observe that those leaders generally hold on to their power by building political connections with those above them or through fear and intimidation rather than by building a loyal and motivated following. In other words, they're the appointed leader but not the accepted leader. These leaders, whether or not they know it, are on shaky ground. People don't like to be coerced into action through fear, and such leaders are always in danger of losing their political clout and being fired, or having their best and brightest disappear out from under them or sabotage their direction.

If you haven't yet read the tutorial on listening at the end of this book, I suggest you do that now. It will give you a good grounding in the tools for pursuing your curiosity.

Curiosity + Listening = The Beginning of Wisdom

True curiosity is powerful, and it's built into all of us. Anyone who has been around a toddler for any length of time can attest to that. The endless "Why?" and "How come?" and "What's that?" are all outward manifestations of that inward engine of curiosity. I see curiosity as the impulse to investigate. For children, that impulse is a powerful, instinctive survival mechanism: the more they understand the environment and the more quickly they do so, the more likely they are to succeed as human beings. Children's insatiable curiosity drives them to learn to speak, eat, walk, understand how to manipulate objects, and learn to interact with other human beings. It leads them to understand what is dangerous and what is safe, what is delicious and what is disgusting, what is useful and what is pointless.

Unfortunately, many of us lose touch with that inborn curiosity as we become adults. We assume we're largely done growing and that we understand our world well enough, thank you very much. Our curiosity is often stifled by others as well: "Don't meddle in things that don't concern you," we're taught; "Don't read ahead," and "Don't question your superiors," and even that "curiosity killed the cat." These are all clear societal messages to stop investigating your environment.

Your core of curiosity is still in there, though. I'm convinced everyone has this core, and I want to help you cultivate it so that you will become a wiser leader.

Try It: Getting Curious

Think of this as curiosity calisthenics.

Think about the last time you were genuinely curious and really wanted to know more or understand more about a situation, a topic, or a person. How did it feel? What did it make you want to do? (You can simply reflect on this or can note your responses in your trusty notebook.) I suspect you might say something like, "It was fun," or, "I was focused," and that what it made you want to do was listen: "I wanted to ask questions" or "I wanted to ask where I could get more information."

Now think of an area where it would be useful for you to be curious, but about which you don't now feel curious. Maybe it's something your spouse really enjoys but you think is silly, or an initiative at work that's going to affect you but you don't really care about. Note your self-talk about this area. I imagine it's along the lines of, "This is boring," or "I don't need to know this."

How could you change your self-talk about this thing in order to engage your curiosity? Write down a revised self-talk message in your notebook that you believe and that will nudge you toward curiosity—for example:

> I wonder if being involved in this initiative could help my
> team in some way.
> I'd love to find out what my wife finds interesting about this.

Once you've engaged your curiosity, use your listening skills to dig into the topic: attend, invite, restate, and question.

#2 Assess Situations Objectively (Fair Witness)

Fair witnessing is the essence of wisdom; it's the quality that people most often reference when they speak of someone as wise.

Wonya Lucas, the president and CEO of TV One, is another wise leader. I recently facilitated a vision and strategy session for the Cable and Telecommunication Association for Marketing, and Wonya is a member of its board. At one point in the discussion, we were talking about how and whether the association should change the focus of some of its offers to better serve its members. One person was highly enthusiastic about how a particular offer would appeal to the membership, and most of the other participants in the session were getting caught up in the person's enthusiasm. I saw Wonya listening carefully, not yet responding. A few minutes later she spoke up, noting that while she agreed that the membership would love the offer, she wasn't sure about their bosses. Ultimately they were the ones who would have to pay for the members to use it, and it might be a harder sell to convince them of the value of it. Her balanced insight changed the flow of the conversation, and the group ended up agreeing on a more robust and universally appealing offer.

I've often seen Wonya be the fair witness for a group; she seems to have a real gift for keeping her objectivity, even when all around her are losing theirs. People rely on this ability in their leaders. We look to them for guidance, and when we don't respect the quality of their insight or don't believe that they can stay objective about important situations, we question their decisions. I don't mean question in the good, I'm-curious-about-why-you-made-that-decision kind of way; I mean question in the sense of not trusting the validity of those decisions and making plans to protect ourselves from their assumed poor outcomes.

When people don't think a leader is wise in this way, a shadow system arises: they make their own assessments and decisions, and contingency plans and second-guessing abound. People spend time and thought focused on how to help the leader see the situation more clearly (without making him or her seem wrong; difficulty in admitting mistakes often accompanies lack of wisdom), or on getting him or her to change unwise decisions that have arisen from that lack of clarity. It saps the organization's energy.

Try It: Put on Your Fair Witness Robes

I'll offer one additional suggestion here to hone your fair witness skills and help you become wiser in every aspect of your life—not just as a leader.

The next time you're faced with an important decision, take a moment to mentally put on your fair witness robes. I mean it: imagine putting on a long white robe and then saying to yourself, "I am now a fair witness." Look at the situation anew from your fair witness vantage point. I've found that doing this automatically shifts my mental focus and allows me to look at the situation more objectively and dispassionately. Notice whether "putting on your robes" changes either the quality or the conclusions of your assessment.

#3 Reflect On and Learn from Their Experience

Let's say you've gotten curious and really listened. You've been a fair witness about what you've seen and heard, and you've taken a step or made a decision or spoken up based on your understanding.

The next step for a wise leader is to notice what happens as a result of his or her actions and use that to learn and improve. This requires two things: first, that you stay curious, stay listening, and stay in fair witness mode (especially if things haven't turned out as you planned) so you can accurately see the outcomes of your words or actions; second, that you learn from what you see.

We often think of learning only as the acquisition of a body of knowledge or a set of skills through instruction or study. In this context, though, I'm referring to another definition of learning: modification of behaviors or beliefs based on experience.

I often see leaders, even those who are wise in other ways, fall down in this area. A few years ago an executive I know was lamenting the failure of her boss, Jerry, to learn from his experience. A colleague of hers, a man named Lawrence, had been misrepresenting his own group's results to Jerry by taking credit for another group's work. Lawrence had done this before, and Jerry had ignored it; the result was conflict, bad feeling, and wasted time and energy between the two functions. It had made people question Jerry's fairness and his insight. Now Lawrence was repeating his behavior, and once again, the boss was turning a blind eye. "Jerry knows how this will turn out," she said to me in frustration. "Why doesn't he stop it?" When I had the opportunity to talk to him a few weeks later, Jerry brushed it off. "It's not that big a deal," he said. "It will sort itself out." This was perhaps a failure of courage but certainly a failure of wisdom.

When a leader isn't seen to reflect on and learn from his or her experience, people question whether that person will be effective in responding to changed circumstances. *Changing circumstance are the true measure of leadership.* If you could just keep doing exactly what made you successful up until now for the rest of your life and be equally successful, I wouldn't even be addressing this topic.

But people know that things change, and that's when a leader earns his or her stripes. Responding to change requires farsightedness, passion, and courage. These attributes serve you in times of change by allowing you to see a possible future, move toward it, and stay the course. But change also requires wisdom—the quality that allows you to shift your actions and your assumptions in response to new experience and new data. In times gone by, this capability could mean life or death for the tribe; if one approach to war or food or shelter didn't work, the leader had better be able to learn from that and adapt or face serious consequences. So we're wired to look for it and to require it in those who lead us.

When someone doesn't learn from experience, it feels dangerous to us: our deepest instincts tell us this means he or she is more likely to lead us all to destruction. We retract our faith and belief and our will to follow, and we try to figure things out for ourselves, as individuals, rather than together with our leader and our teammates. We lose the power that arises from unity.

How We Learn from Experience

Over the years, I've noticed that those who are best at learning from experience have positive self-talk about their ability to do so. They also generally have developed a simple process for reflecting on what's happened and identifying those things that could be changed to get a better outcome going forward.

I saw Kathy Dore do this again and again during the years when she was a client. I noticed that when something didn't work the way she'd hoped—a program, a sales effort, a business process—she'd sit down with her team and have an honest postmortem. She'd ask, "Why didn't this work?" or "What held us back from even greater success?" Then she'd help guide the conversation so that people could discover the elements of the effort most likely to be the source of any problems. Once they had gotten clearer on the shape of the problem, she'd ask, "What do we need to do differently next time to make this work [or make it work even better]?" And I know from speaking to her that her self-talk about this process was generally hopeful and practical: "We can figure this out. We can make this better."

As a result, Kathy built strong, loyal, capable teams that deeply respected and supported her as their leader. Together they were able to build new businesses, turn around failing businesses, and drive existing businesses to achieve much higher levels of success.

Try It: Become a Better Learner

Small children are not only curious; they are also amazing learners. I've been spending a good bit of time with my baby granddaughter, Hannah, lately, and she is (like all other babies) a relentless learner. She's continually trying new things, and whenever something doesn't work, she immediately tries something else. The activity that follows is focused on helping you regain that wonderful learner's mind:

1. Think about and write in your notebook the last time you did something that didn't work out well. It could be personal or professional: a date you went on, a project you proposed, a conversation you had or didn't have with a colleague or friend.

2. What was your immediate reaction? I suggest you check off the reactions you had from the list below (you can pick more than one—and be honest):

   ❑ Denial or rationalization ("It was okay. No, really!")
   ❑ Blame ("It was the other person's fault.")
   ❑ Excuses ("I didn't have enough information," or "The timing was bad," or something else.)
   ❑ Embarrassment ("What will people think of me?")
   ❑ Self-flagellation ("I'm SUCH an idiot!!)
   ❑ Anger ("#$%&*@#!")
   ❑ Disappointment ("I really wanted that to work.")
   ❑ Frustration ("Grrrrr.")
   ❑ Curiosity ("Hmmm, what happened there?")
   ❑ Determination ("I can do this better next time.")

3. Review your picks. I'm convinced that toddlers don't waste any time on the first five (denial, blame, excuses, embarrassment, and self-flagellation). And though they definitely experience the next three (anger, disappointment, and frustration), they quickly move on to the last two: curiosity and determination. It's what makes them such gifted learners.

The first five reactions will inhibit your ability to learn from experience. If you checked any of them, I imagine you had negative, unhelpful self-talk supporting those reactions. Think about how you could change your self-talk to help you get to curiosity and determination. Write that revised self-talk in your notebook to help anchor it in your head. For instance, if your original self-talk supported anger and blame, you might revise it to be something like this:

> When things don't go the way I expect them to, it's tough not to take out my frustration on somebody else. But I don't want to do that: it generally makes things worse. I'll breathe deeply and focus on using my fair witness skills.

Now think about how you might have behaved differently as a result of using that more learning-focused self-talk—for example, "I might have tried alternatives"; "I might have asked someone more skilled for advice"; "I might have explored to get clearer about what exactly didn't work." Write down some of those behaviors for future reference; this is how you'll build your own capability to reflect on and learn from your experience.

#4 See Patterns, and Share Their Insights with Others

About ten years ago, I was conducting a planning session for another TV industry association, and, again, Wonya was a member of the planning team. The group, Women in Cable Telecommunications (WICT), had recently worked with us to clarify its mission and vision and was in the process of creating a clear strategic and tactical plan to move toward the vision. One of the strategies focused on their offer: "Provide leadership development offerings tailored to meet the needs of each member." As we were discussing this strategy and how to make it a reality, the group got stuck on how to assess their current offerings relative to their existing members, so they'd know where the holes in their offer were and begin to fill them.

It was a complex conversation: existing offers, possible offers, a variety of members and constituencies, a variety of needs. As I listened to the conversation, I noticed that many, if not most, of the people in the room were overly focused on a particular aspect of the problem and not seeing the whole picture. I encouraged them to try to see the overall situation—what I call "pulling back the camera."

Wonya, who had been primarily listening and asking questions up to this point, suddenly sat up straight. "What about this?" she said. "We could create a matrix of members and their needs. On the vertical dimension we could list our different member groups; the horizontal dimension could be possible leadership needs. Then we can fill in the blanks with existing offerings that meet a particular need for a particular member, and we'll see where the holes are." There was a moment of silence as everyone thought this through, and then the whole group burst into spontaneous laughter and applause. "And we'll call it the Wonya Lucas commemorative matrix," someone joked. Wonya's idea broke the logjam and provided a way for everyone to start thinking about the problem more holistically. WICT still uses a version of the matrix to help make sure its offers best meet its members' needs.

I love this example and use it often: it's a great, simple demonstration of this aspect of wisdom. Wonya was able to step back from the details, see the larger pattern formed by those details, and share her insights with the group.

This capability definitely builds on the first two: you have to get curious, listen, and be a fair witness as a starting point. But then you also need to pull back the camera.

How to Pull Back the Camera

Imagine a scene in a movie. The camera is pulled in tight, and all you see is a lamp on a table. It looks pretty ordinary. Now the camera pans back, and you see that the lamp and the table are sitting in a completely empty room, with no other furniture, no rugs, no curtains on the windows. Now it's not quite so ordinary. The camera pans back again, through the window and out to the street. Now you see the whole house; there's a real estate sign on the front lawn with a "sold" sticker pasted across it. Suddenly it all makes sense.

Pulling back the camera brings more information into the frame, giving you the context you need to understand what you're seeing. When the camera is pulled in tight, it's easy to make inaccurate assumptions about what you're seeing; small things can seem much more central and important to the whole than they really are.

I've noticed over the years that when people say someone is "too tactical," they almost invariably mean that person operates with the camera pulled in too close to their own piece of the action. Leaders, to be wise, need to step back mentally so they can see the whole picture.

Here's another example. Years ago, I was at the Museum of Modern Art in New York City. When I walked into the room where Monet's single-panel *Water Lilies* hangs, I was first struck by its size: it's over six feet high and almost twenty feet long. You have to stand across the room to take it all in at once. From a distance, you can see how wonderfully Monet captured the tranquility of light-suffused water, floating water lilies, and clouds overhead. But when you move in close to the painting, the pattern dissolves, and all you see is a collection of seemingly random brush strokes in a variety of colors: your "camera" is pulled in too close to make sense of it.

Unwise leaders tend to get caught in the brushstrokes. They pull their mental camera in close, or direct it toward just one part of the enterprise, and they come to shortsighted conclusions based on their too-tight perspective. Let's say that a particular company isn't hitting its sales targets, and the head of sales is trying to understand and solve the problem. If she pulls in the camera too close, she might focus on only one or two formerly high-performing salespeople who are missing their targets. Just looking at that one part of the situation, she could assume any number of things: that they've somehow lost their edge or are slacking off; that firing them will solve the problem; or, conversely, that if she really leans on them, they'll get better. Based on those assumptions, she might let them go, offer them training, or read them the riot act.

But if instead she pulls back the camera and looks at the overall sales situation, she might see that the new product line the two salespeople are now responsible for selling isn't performing as promised because of a manufacturing glitch. The high return level is affecting both current sales numbers and their customers' willingness to reorder. The broader view gives a very different perspective and will almost surely lead her to a different, more effective response.

Try It: Finding Patterns

Pulling back your mental camera in order to see the important patterns in a situation is a developable skill. And like any other skill, it requires practice. It's also an area where it's really helpful to have a teacher.

First, think of someone you know well and think is really good at seeing patterns. This person can usually get to the heart of a problem or can see the most important aspects of a situation. This is someone you think of as wise. Ask this person if he or she will be your coach in learning to develop this capability. (You're welcome to share this chapter by way of explanation. I'll almost guarantee you it will make sense to them.) I encourage you to take advantage of your patterns coach in three ways:

- Ask for examples of times when he or she has been able to see the key elements of a situation when others haven't (like Wonya's matrix example). Have the person walk you through his or her mental process for seeing all the critical factors at once and pulling out a pattern. Listen carefully.
- Bring the person a situation you're wrestling with and ask him or her to discuss with you the critical elements. Notice if he or she asks you questions that cause you to pull back the camera to look at the situation more broadly; when you do, notice what new information comes into your "viewfinder."
- When you believe you've seen a powerful pattern in a situation, bring your conclusion to your coach and share it as simply as possible: "In this situation, I think the key factors are X, Y and Z." Ask for your coach's feedback. Pay special attention to the questions the person asks you in order to build his or her own understanding of the situation. And if this person disagrees with your assessment, get clear on what he or she is seeing differently and why.

Working with another person in this way will help you grow in both aspects of this part of wisdom: you'll get better at seeing patterns, and you'll get better at articulating them. Plus, you'll have lots of chances to exercise your curiosity!

#5 Act Based on What They Believe Is Morally Right

This is the bottom line of wisdom. Wise leaders, in my experience, always factor what they believe is right in the moral sense into their deliberations, conclusions, and decisions. Thousands of books have been written over the centuries about right and wrong, including pretty much every scripture ever set to paper; this is not one of them. I'm not proposing a particular morality. I'm simply saying that wise leaders have a clear moral compass: they know what they consider to be right or wrong and make effort to be true to that compass.

A number of years ago, when Kathy Dore was president of Entertainment Services for Rainbow Media Holdings, running Bravo, IFC, and IFC Entertainment, she oversaw the sale of Bravo to NBC. Mergers and acquisitions are by their nature complex and fraught with countless opportunities for wisdom—or the lack thereof. In one area, Kathy had an important choice about which path to take: the agreements to be made about who would stay with Rainbow and who would go to NBC with the sale. In situations like this, I've often watched executives maneuver to keep the "good" people for themselves and arrange it so that any less talented or committed employees end up going to the purchaser.

Kathy refused to operate this way. She worked closely with her executive team to make sure that the staff assignments were as fair as possible and that Bravo would have the people needed to continue to grow and thrive and Rainbow would keep the folks it was most appropriate for them to keep. She also spent a lot of time thinking about the people for whom there wasn't a reasonable spot in either entity and how to transition them out with as much support and care as possible.

It was clear to me throughout this process that she was making a conscious choice to approach the situation in this extremely fair witness way. In her mind, this was the appropriate way for her to behave as a leader, and therefore this was how she behaved.

The other thing I noticed was her lack of self-righteousness. She made what for her was the moral choice, but she didn't announce or publicize it, or point out how "good" she was being. She just did it. And that kind of wise behavior bears wonderful fruit in support and loyalty. At the end of the transition, they had a big party for everyone who was leaving, and Kathy spoke to the group, saying, "Always remember the friends you've made here, always remember the good work you've done here, and always remember that you've made a difference." When Kathy left Rainbow a few years later to go to Canwest, her employees gave her a bowl engraved with those words.

This final element of wisdom is particularly important to followers. If we see that someone has a clear moral code and consistently adheres to it, we have faith that he or she won't sell us or the enterprise down the river—literally or figuratively. Even if we don't always agree with this person's conclusions, it's hugely reassuring to know that he or she is striving to do the right thing. It's also inspiring. Most of us want to believe that businesses can do well while doing right, and wise leaders show us that's possible. It's attractive and motivating to both the people who work for that leader and to those who use or buy the company's goods or services.

Try It: Setting Your Moral Compass

In order to demonstrate this aspect of wisdom, you have to be clear on your own morality. This doesn't happen all at once: new situations arise over time that cause us to refine or expand our definitions of what is right in a business context. However, setting aside time to reflect on and get clear about your own core values will provide a firm foundation for being a wise leader.

As you clarify your values, it's also important to think about how those values translate into your day-to-day life: we call those your "demonstrated beliefs." Use the questions that follow as thought starters. Don't try to answer them now or all at once; each one covers a lot of moral territory. Read one, and go away and reflect on it for as long as you need to do so. What do you really believe is right in this area? How will you act in support of that belief? How will you demonstrate it in your daily life? When you've come to conclusions for a given question about what you believe and how you can demonstrate it, write them in your notebook.

- What must a leader do and not do in interacting with his or her employees?
- What might your boss ask you to do for the company that wouldn't be okay with you?
- What kind of information is a company morally obligated to share with its stakeholders?
- What would you *not* give up or compromise in order to make a great deal of money (whatever "a great deal" means to you)?
- What kind of company information, if you discovered it, would you feel morally obligated to share with the authorities?
- What is okay and not okay to do or say in order to make a sale?

In leader folktales, the hero always develops wisdom. He may not be wise at the start, but he learns to follow the wizard's advice, see the patterns in the puzzles before him, and make the moral choice. You can develop wisdom too, and it will help you become not only an accepted leader—one who others gladly follow—but also a high-quality human being in every aspect of your life.

Core Ideas

Wisdom is the reflective attribute that balances farsightedness, passion, and courage. When a leader is wise, people respect the quality of that leader's thinking and decisions, and they feel respected by the quality of his or her attention. If the leader isn't wise, people will second-guess decisions, hesitate to follow, and ultimately look for wiser counsel.

Leaders who are *wise*:

- *Are deeply curious; they listen.* Like children, they have a will to explore and understand what they discover.

- *Assess situations objectively (fair witness).* They make every effort to see people and situations as accurately as possible.

- *Reflect on and learn from their experience.* Whether things go well or badly, they glean everything they can to improve going forward.

- *See patterns and share their insights with others.* They pull back the camera to see the core elements, and they say what they see.

- *Act based on what they believe is morally right.* They're clear about their own moral code, and they live by it.

SEVEN

Generous

Just then, the same ancient crone stepped from the dusky shadows, leaning on her gnarled stick. "Have you a coin for an old woman?" she asked in her thin voice, holding out her wrinkled hand.

"Yes, certainly," said the youngest brother, dipping into his little purse and selecting a small silver coin. "It's not much, but you're welcome to it."

She took the coin and hid it in the folds of her ragged gown. "And have you bread to share with a poor old woman?" she asked, holding out her hand again.

"Yes, and you are welcome to it too," said the boy, breaking off and handing her a chunk of his simple brown bread.

"So be it," said the old woman, her voice stronger. The youngest brother watched, amazed, as the old woman grew and changed, becoming young and beautiful. She smiled at the boy, her face kind. Raising her stick, now straight and shining, she touched the lip of the well.

When Danny Meyer smiles, other people smile too. His good humor and hopefulness are highly infectious. Danny and I are walking along a Manhattan street, coming back to his office from a Webcast we've just taped for Forbes.com about how to be a good people manager. Danny's talking about the speaking gigs he's been doing lately, and he's excited. I notice people looking at him and breaking into spontaneous grins; it's fun just to be around his energy. The good vibes continue when we get back to the Union Square Hospitality Group (USHG) offices, the company that Danny founded and of which he is now CEO. People seem genuinely glad to see him. As he walks toward his office, each little encounter is full of life: a shared smile, a brief greeting, a moment spent telling someone that he liked a graphic she had created, a quick question and response with one of his partners.

We've been working with Danny and his team for twenty years; they're our longest client relationship. When I began developing this leadership model in the mid-1990s, Danny was the first person I thought of as an exemplar of the generous leader. And as I watch him make his way through the office, I see it again: Danny is generous with all the things a leader has to offer: time, attention, praise, resources, trust, information, knowledge, and, perhaps most notable, power.

I've watched Danny's business grow over the past two decades from a single restaurant to a world-spanning array of eating establishments. We first started working with USHG when the group was about to open its second restaurant, Gramercy Tavern, and now USHG runs fine dining restaurants, barbecue/jazz joints, a catering company, fast food emporia, and upscale concessions at major sports arenas. Although these venues are hugely disparate in terms of menu, pricing, and locale, all of them have at their core Danny's credo of "enlightened hospitality," which is all about generosity: taking care of each other, their guests, their vendors, the community, and the shareholders.

During that arc of growth, I've watched Danny share the wealth, literally and metaphorically, with hundreds of people. They are not only his partners, who have been there throughout the journey and shared in the company's success, growing enormously as professionals in the process, but also lots of frontline employees—people who started out five or ten or fifteen years ago as waiters or kitchen staff and have gotten the chance to manage staff, learn operations, and run restaurants. Danny is a living example of the power of generosity: he is almost continuously giving, and consistently getting back even more than he gives.

What Is True Generosity?

We tend to think of generous people as those who share material wealth: giving to charity, buying expensive gifts, or taking the in-laws out for dinner. In business, we think of generous leaders as those who provide a way for their people to share materially in the success of the company— through raises, profit sharing, or a bonus system. All of these things can be good, but they are only part of true generosity. As I've noted with Danny, truly generous leaders share the wealth on many levels. For example, they are quick to give others credit for their good efforts and new ideas. They're also generous with their knowledge, sharing information with those who need it and teaching others around them how to do what they themselves do well. They are generous with their faith in people; they tend to assume best intent (although they are not naive) and believe people are generally innocent until proven guilty.

Perhaps most important, they are generous with power. The generous leader, having provided the information necessary for success, gives people the authority and autonomy to act on that information. A leader who is fully generous shares both the power to make decisions and the responsibility for dealing with the consequences of those decisions. She shares the resources needed to execute on the power she shares and the insight and support necessary for people to recover from mistakes and failure. Finally, she is generous with feedback. She takes the time to notice what her staff are doing or not doing, think about what's great and what's not, and share with them her observations.

What About in Times of Scarcity?

As we've worked with leaders during these last few years of economic shakiness, we often get pushback about generosity. *How can we be generous when resources are thin?* they ask. I'm convinced that question arises from a narrow definition of generosity and a narrow understanding of what people most want from their leaders.

Bosses tend to err on the side of thinking that what's most important to workers is material generosity: high wages, lush benefits, big offices. And while everyone wants a living wage, reasonable working conditions, and insurance coverage, research has shown again and again that what employees most want, and what most effectively creates a committed and productive workforce, are things like appreciation, interesting work, being included, being trusted, having opportunities for individual growth, and flexible schedules. In other words, they most want their leaders to be generous with acknowledgment, responsibility, information, trust, and openness to new ways of working. And fortunately for leaders, that sort of generosity is possible in good times and bad.

In fact, being generous in that way can often make up for a temporary lack of ability to be generous with resources. In the depths of this last recession, at the beginning of 2009, a client of ours called a town hall meeting with his whole company, about 250 employees. He told them that revenues had really taken a hit (the banking industry formed a big part of its customer base). He let everyone know they were making immediate efforts to diversify their client base and that they felt they'd be back on track by the following year. He said that he was 100 percent committed to not laying anyone off but noted that in order to keep that promise, they were going to have to forgo yearly bonuses and put a freeze on raises and promotions. If it got worse before it got better, they might have to institute some temporary wage cuts. He said that the same cost-cutting measures applied to everyone in the organization, including him. He also shared that he was going to take a voluntary 15 percent pay cut for the year. Finally, he told everyone in the organization that they were welcome to look at a high-level profit-and-loss statement to see how the cuts would balance lost revenue and allow some modest investment in sales and marketing.

The employees weren't thrilled, of course, but his generosity with information, his generosity in committing to retaining all the employees, and his personal generosity in taking a hit in advance of everyone else were meaningful to people. The company squeaked through the year, and by the third quarter of 2010 sales were largely back on track. Only one key person left, and our client believes that his folks' generous response (in time, collaboration, creativity, and commitment) was largely responsible for their fairly quick return to profitability.

Generous leadership makes people feel capable, included, and motivated to succeed. It also makes them feel generous themselves. A generous leader is a powerful role model and catalyst for an open, honest, supportive organization.

How to Be Generous

Generosity is in some ways easier to identify and cultivate than some of the other attributes. It's still helpful to have a handful of specific behaviors to focus on if this is one of the areas where you need to develop as a leader.

Leaders Who Are Generous

1. Assume positive intent
2. Share power and authority
3. Share what they know
4. Freely give credit, praise, and reward
5. Provide the resources necessary to succeed

It's especially important, as you assess yourself in this attribute, to be a fair witness. Because it's embarrassing to think that we might not be generous (nobody wants to be considered a jerk, a miser, or selfish), it's easy to sort of zip past this one, thinking, *Oh yeah, sure, I'm good at that*.

But really reflect on each of the five behaviors and ask yourself, "How consistent am I in doing this?" You may believe in all these things, but do you actually behave this way? Recently I began coaching an executive who truly believed he was generous. He does have a really good heart, but he wasn't sharing power and authority or assuming positive intent, and so his people didn't see him as a generous leader. (He's taking steps to improve now that he's more aware of his behavior and how it has affected others.)

So assess yourself as accurately as possible (this is a definitely a stretch for your fair witness muscles). Use a scale of 1 to 3 to rate yourself in these behaviors, where 1 is, "I don't do this consistently; it's definitely a growth area"; 2 is, "This is a strength of mine; I do it consistently"; and 3 is, "I am unusually skilled and consistent in this area; it's a key strength." Then explore the elements where you could use some help.

#1 Assume Positive Intent

I worked with someone for many years who seemed to operate on the assumption that everyone was out to get her and her company. When others failed to share important information with her, for instance, she didn't assume that they had forgotten or didn't know that she needed it. Rather, her automatic assumption tended to be that they had intentionally withheld the information because they were trying to make her life difficult, or wanted her to fail, or were simply incompetent.

She and I spent a lot of time talking about the power of assuming positive intent, but she wasn't able to change her mind-set. I think she believed that assuming negative intent (although she wouldn't agree that's what she was doing; she called it being "prudent") protected her from getting hurt or being taken by surprise.

Unfortunately, a great many leaders seem to share this point of view. I've seen otherwise good leaders run off the rails because they so often assume others have negative intent.

Here's an example. Many years ago, I was engaged to coach the head of marketing in a client company. Allan, I'll call him, was extremely creative and personally productive; I'd observed him as being farsighted, passionate, and even courageous. But his lack of wisdom and, especially, generosity had damaged his relationships with his peers and his team along the way. His boss, the CEO, wanted to see if he could be helped to improve, and Allan seemed open to coaching.

When we do executive coaching, we conduct confidential interviews with six to eight people who work closely with the person to be coached (we work together with the coachee to select this interview pool). These colleagues give us a good sense of how those around this person see him or her.

It became clear to me as I spoke to his interviewees that Allan was consistently making negative assumptions about people's intentions and that he didn't see all the problematic results of his negative, limited assumptions. For instance, he decided early on that a new colleague of his, Claire, was ill intended; he thought she was egotistical and self-focused and that her actions were aimed at controlling and excluding others from discussions or decisions. Because he had such faith in his negative assumptions about Claire, all his interactions with her were stiff and guarded.

I had the chance to facilitate a meeting with him, his peers, and the CEO before we started our formal coaching engagement, and I got to see the impact of his negative assumptions firsthand. The group was having a pretty wide-ranging discussion about the potential marketing campaign and sales plan for a new TV series, and everyone had been weighing in. But when Claire expressed her point of view, Allan snapped at her, "Hey, this isn't even part of your job. I don't know why you think you should be able to make that decision." She looked taken aback and started to defend herself. Before I could step in to untangle it, the CEO sighed and said, "Allan, back off. We're just talking." Allan subsided, but I could tell by the look on his face that he thought, *They're all in this together; they're trying to take away my power.*

It turned out he was acting in the same way with his own team: he would assume they were trying to undermine his authority when they merely disagreed with him and making plans behind his back if they met without telling him. Without meaning to, he had created a strong atmosphere of resentment and uncertainty around him: people walked on eggshells for fear he would take the most innocent actions in a negative way.

The coaching was only modestly helpful. Allen really wanted to succeed, but it was tough for him to change. He had spent a lifetime cultivating the assumption of negative intent as a protective mechanism, and it was difficult for him to let it go.

Another generous leader with whom I've worked for many years, and for whom I have great affection, is Doug Herzog, president of Viacom Entertainment Group. Doug is much more likely to assume positive than negative intent: he believes that people generally want to do good work and that you should hire smart, capable people and assume that they'll then be smart and capable. I've noticed over the years that most people really like working for him: they tend to blossom in the sun of his regard and feel motivated to fulfill his positive expectations. Of course, sometimes people don't fulfill his expectations, and then he can be disappointed, and sometimes he even has to let them go. But the vast majority of the time, I've seen his hopefulness about people bear fruit.

At one point, Doug was having some difficulties with one of his direct reports. Joe was running programming for one of the channels Doug manages, and while he was creative and smart, he was uncommunicative and hard to read. Rather than assuming that Joe had some hidden agenda or was being secretive, Doug assumed that he simply didn't understand how his lack of communication was affecting those around him. He offered Joe an executive coach; Joe took advantage of the opportunity and improved his communication and his focus on teaming with others. Now, almost ten years later, Joe is running the network, and he and Doug have a strong and positive working relationship.

That's why it's important for leaders to assume positive intent. When the leader is generous in his or her assumptions, everyone feels good. Generosity creates an open environment that supports risk taking and allows people to do their best work. If I'm an employee and I see that my leader has high positive expectations and believes I can meet them, I'm likely to do everything in my power to make that true.

Try It: Generous Self-Talk

The assumption of positive or negative intent resides in how you talk to yourself about situations. Let's use your self-talk skills to help you create a generous mind-set.

Most of us have little self-talk mantras that support the assumption of negative intent—things that we habitually say to ourselves about others' supposed negative motivations. You can probably discover yours by reflecting on what you tend to say to yourself when a conversation or interaction doesn't go well. It could be anything: "He just doesn't like me," "She's threatened by me," "Those people are always trying to make things tough for me," "They don't care about quality."

What are yours? I suggest you write down your most common negative intent mantras in your notebook.

Now pick out the one you believe you default to most often. How could you change that self-talk to support the assumption of positive intent? Remember that it has to be something you believe. So you wouldn't change, "He doesn't like me," to, "I'm his favorite person." But you might change it to, "I don't know how he feels about me. I'm assuming a lot based on the fact that he hasn't yet returned my phone call." That's believable and more likely to allow the assumption of positive intent. I find it gratifying to cross out my unhelpful self-talk and write my revised "assuming positive intent" (or at least neutral intent) self-talk beneath it.

Assuming that others are basically well intended toward you until you have clear evidence that they are not is the leadership equivalent of innocent until proven guilty. Yes, you may occasionally be caught off-guard by someone who really is deceptive or out to get you. But the negative fallout from that will generally be hugely outweighed by the positive outcomes from the justified positive assumptions you make about the majority of those you lead.

#2 Share Power and Authority

Danny Meyer is a truly wonderful example of this. A few years ago, I helped him and his partners restructure their business; it had grown so much that they all needed to expand their roles. They brought in one new person: a guy who had skills and experience that they all acknowledged they needed and didn't have. But other than that, the focus was on helping Danny and his four long-time partners figure out how to manage this much larger company in a way that made best use of their skills and spoke to their hopes and ambitions.

One of the partners wanted to run part of the business, and Danny wasn't sure he was the right person for the job (I also had my doubts). But Danny decided to give him a shot: he really wanted to do it and made a compelling case for it. Most important, though, once Danny had made his decision, he backed it up completely with his actions; he didn't get in his partner's way by hovering or second-guessing his decisions. And that part of the business has since grown dramatically under this executive's leadership.

What Gets in the Way?

As you might suspect, having self-talk that supports delegation is critical. If you're saying things to yourself like, "No one can do this as well as I do," or "I can't trust others to care about quality," it's deeply unlikely that you'll delegate well or completely. The good news is that you can also talk to yourself in a way that supports delegation because it's simply another application of your ever-deepening self-talk skills.

Nevertheless, there's another potential impediment in this area. In my experience, the majority of leaders don't know how to delegate well. They may hand the responsibility to the other person and walk away, or they may stay deeply involved throughout even if the other person supposedly owns it, or they may jump in and out of the work as it occurs to them or seems important. None of these works very well, and the third approach is particularly unsettling and demoralizing.

How to Share Power Well

In another book of mine, *Growing Great Employees*, I devote an entire chapter to the art and practice of delegation, and I invite you to read it if this is an area where you know you need improvement. I've created a more condensed version of our delegation model in this section that offers the basic skills for more effectively sharing power and authority.

First, a definition is important. In my mind, *delegation* means transferring to an employee the responsibility for an area of work. It's not just assigning tasks. This transfer may be quick or gradual, depending on the employee's experience and learning style, and the area of work may be large or small. It may also be a permanent transfer, as with a promotion or a new job responsibility, or a temporary one—for instance, completing a project or working on a time-limited cross-functional team.

It's your responsibility to make the hand-off well and skillfully, and it's the employee's responsibility to be there to receive it.

The delegation model has three important components:

- *Prepare.* Before you meet with the employee, take some time to define the area of work you want to delegate and the levels of autonomy appropriate for this employee in doing this work. This will give you a chance to clarify the size and shape of this responsibility, so that you can communicate it clearly to the employee. Defining levels of autonomy will allow you to decide the appropriate levels of autonomy for various elements of the work.
- *Discuss and agree.* When you meet with your employee, first share the area of work and make sure there's mutual understanding and agreement. Then you'll share your levels-of-autonomy preparation in order to define the transfer of responsibility from you to him or her. This is the most critical part of the conversation; it allows you and the employee to discuss and agree on how the hand-off will take place over time. Finally, you'll ask the employee to put it all together by creating a document that summarizes what you've agreed on.
- *Support.* No matter how well you complete the first two steps, it's unlikely that the transfer of responsibility will work without the third step. In this step, you both honor the commitments you've made in the delegation conversation and offer the employee feedback about how he or she is doing relative to the agreed-on responsibility. Most

important, you work to build the employee's capability, and therefore his or her autonomy, so that ultimately this person is fully responsible for this area, with minimal involvement from you.

Effective delegation is the best way for you to share power and authority. It allows employees to demonstrate increasing levels of competence; you can then respond by offering them increasing levels of autonomy. They become more independent and capable, and you'll be freed to take on new, higher-level responsibilities as well. When you operate as a generous leader, your people benefit and respond.

THE PREPARE STEP   The first part of this step is to define the area of responsibility. Ask yourself, "What is the scope of the area I want to delegate?" You want to define the area as a whole, so that the employee gets a sense of the big picture. Often people make the mistake of inundating the employee with step-by-step specifics when trying to explain a new responsibility. Remember that you're not teaching the person how to do the responsibility at this point; you're simply introducing the idea of taking it on. In order to avoid going into too much detail, here are some of the topics to talk about during this first conversation:

- A summary description of the responsibility
- Key people involved and with whom your employee will need to interact
- A recent history of this project or responsibility (for example, how it's being done now and by whom)
- Important benchmarks, cycles, or other time frames
- Skills needed (you can let the employee know you'll be available to coach as necessary)
- Results or standards expected

As you think through this, I suggest writing down these important aspects of the area of responsibility to use as a memory aid when sharing this information with your employee.

Once you've thought through what this area of responsibility entails, you turn to the second part of the step: defining the levels of autonomy. Begin by drawing a continuum (Figure 7.1). Now place each part of the project or responsibility along the continuum in the appropriate spot, based on your level of confidence in this person's ability in that area.

Let's say you're an account manager, and you're delegating a client account to an employee. You know she has had experience in dealing with high-level people; you've seen her in action and have been impressed. You put "client relations" at the far right of the continuum, meaning you have confidence in her ability to handle this aspect of the account. At the same time, you know that this person isn't so good with detailed follow-through, so you put "detail orientation" at the far left of the continuum. (Figure 7.2 shows the completed continuum.) A low level of confidence may arise from knowing this person isn't strong in this area, as in this case, or from not having seen this person perform in this area, and therefore not knowing his or her capabilities.

Figure 7.1   Levels of Autonomy

Levels of My Confidence / Employee's Autonomy

Low   High

Figure 7.2   An Example: Delegating a Client Account

Levels of My Confidence / Employee's Autonomy

Low   High

Detail Orientation   *Client Relations*

- Review and provide feedback on client communications before they go out

- Go over to-dos from client calls to agree on next steps

- Monthly updates

- Troubleshooting as requested

After you arrange the key aspects of the responsibility along the continuum, note how you want to interact with your employee in each element. Where you have high confidence, you'll offer more autonomy and minimal oversight—for example "monthly updates" and "trouble-shooting as requested."

Where you have less confidence, you offer less autonomy: more frequent interaction, a voice in decision making, and opportunities for coaching, for example. "Review and provide feedback on client communications before they go out" is a useful safety net when you're not confident about someone's detail orientation, as is "Go over 'to-dos' from client calls to agree on next steps."

Note that these proposed left-side interactions are also excellent starting points for development. Your goal, in the areas on the low end, is to provide the support the person needs in order to improve—in effect, to "move to the right." You eventually want to be able to fully delegate, so your goal is to end up with a high level of confidence and autonomy in every aspect of this responsibility. Then you will have truly shared the power.

By defining interactions with an appropriate level of autonomy in each key element of the work you're delegating, you can avoid the primary pitfall of delegation: the one-size-fits-all approach. Most managers pick just one way of approaching delegation—high confidence/autonomy, or low confidence/autonomy—and use it in delegating every element of every responsibility for every employee. We've all seen or heard of examples: the manager who hands new employees a huge stack of files and says (in effect), "Good luck. I have great faith in you. Let me know if you need anything"; or the manager who checks every word of every report, no matter how capable or experienced the employee.

Using the continuum approach allows you to delegate in a way that works for every employee, no matter his or her current level of experience or skill. It also supports moving toward full delegation of responsibility over time, in a practical way, as your confidence (and the employee's) grows.

Try It: Preparing to Delegate

Here is a chance to try this out in your role as a leader. Select an actual project or area of responsibility you want to delegate. We'll work through the whole model using this situation.

Define the Area of Responsibility

In your notebook, define the work you'd like to delegate. What big picture information does this employee need in order to understand what's involved, and to succeed in taking on this responsibility? Remember to focus more on defining the overall area of responsibility than on the details of how to go about it. Here's an example:

> Project-managing the yearly company sales event. This requires coordinating all the people, materials, and efforts involved; managing the budget; working closely with the head of sales to make sure it's in line with what she wants. It's not about creating the content—sales will do that—but coordinating everything else in making it a success.

After you've created your overview of the area you want to delegate, check it again to make sure it offers a reasonably complete picture.

Define Levels of Autonomy

1. Draw the continuum in your notebook, and arrange the key elements of the project or responsibility along it according to your level of confidence in this person's ability to complete a given aspect of the work.
2. For each element on the continuum, define the initial level of interaction and oversight you'd like to have with your employee. Focus on offering the appropriate level of autonomy for each element, given your current level of confidence.

Here's another continuum example, based on the project management delegation above:

Levels of My Confidence / Employee's Autonomy

Low   High

Budgeting

I'll offer templates from previous years, and we'll build this year's together.

Project timelines

We'll review at the beginning to clarify key milestones, and then I'll ask for updates.

Working with head of sales

Share any advice and insights I have.
Encourage her to come to me with questions.

When you've completed the continuum for your own delegation topic, review what you've written in your notebook to make sure the interactions you've proposed toward the left side will provide the initial support needed to develop the employee's capabilities in these areas.

THE DISCUSS/AGREE STEP   When you're satisfied with your definitions of the area of responsibility and the levels of autonomy, it's time to share them with your employee. Your goal is for the employee to leave this discussion feeling clear about what's being requested and how the two of you will work together, being competent to take on this responsibility, and feeling supported to succeed and to move toward full delegation. In order to make sure that all happens, we suggest the following:

1. Offer context.
2. Discuss the area of responsibility.
3. Discuss the levels of autonomy
4. Put it all together.

1. *Offer context.* Too often managers delegate on the fly: "Say, Janet, why don't you take care of this from now on!" We recommend you start the delegation conversation by letting your employee know that you have something important (and positive) to discuss and by making sure he or

she has the time and energy to focus on the conversation. Then give a few sentences of an overview: what the topic is (delegation) and why you want to delegate this responsibility—that is, how it will be good for the employee, for you, and for the organization.

2. *Discuss the area of responsibility.* Your goal here is to make the discussion truly two-way, so that you know the employee understands what you're asking and that you've come to a real agreement. Start by sharing the definition of the project or area of responsibility that you created in the prepare step, above. Use your notes to help you paint a reasonably complete picture, without going into too much detail. Then invite the employee's response; this is your chance to make sure the conversation is two-way. Ask real curiosity-based questions (another use for your listening skills) like, "So, what's your initial reaction?" or "What do you think about taking on this responsibility?" Once the employee is engaged in responding, clarify any areas of misunderstanding or hesitation, and reach agreement on the basic premise—that is, make sure that the employee is ready and willing to take on this responsibility.

3. *Discuss levels of autonomy.* This part of the conversation is uncharted territory for most people. You most likely haven't used the levels-of-autonomy approach in delegating previously, and it's probably unfamiliar to your employee as well. Because it's new for both of you, it needs to be done carefully in order to yield the results you want. I'd suggest using the same basic steps you use to discuss the area of responsibility, above:

- *Share your continuum.* First, let your employee know the principle behind this approach: that you want an initial level of involvement that will be most helpful to him or her and that will allow you to build confidence, and therefore delegate responsibility more fully, as quickly as possible. Once this is clear, walk through your continuum with the employee. We suggest you start at the high side of the continuum to let your employee know where you have the most confidence and reinforce your message about wanting to have everything end up to the right.

- *Invite the employee's response.* Again, use your listening skills to invite the employee into the conversation. Be especially sensitive to areas where the employee may have a different sense of his or her own competence (either higher or lower) than you do. If the person believes he or she is more capable in some area, you can say something like, "I invite you to demonstrate that to me. I'd love to be able to move our interactions in this area to a higher level of autonomy as quickly as possible." If the person has less confidence in his or her ability in a given area than you do (this often happens with managers who have a past habit of overdelegating), be willing to start more to the left on the continuum in your interactions until both you and the employee feel comfortable with a higher level of autonomy.
- *Reach agreement.* Come to an agreement about how you'll initially work together in each aspect of this responsibility. Make sure that the employee is both supported and allowed to stretch.

4. *Put it all together.* Finally, ask the employee to summarize in writing all that you've discussed and agreed based on any documents you've shared and any revisions you've made together. This will serve three purposes: it helps the employee take ownership for the process, allows you to see whether you have the same understanding, and gives both of you a stake in the ground to refer to as you work toward complete delegation in this area.

Try It: The Delegation Conversation

Now you'll plan to have the conversation. I suggest you set up your notebook to go through the entire exercise.

- Note the date by which you'll have this conversation with your employee.
- Offer context. Make a few notes about how you intend to set up the conversation verbally with the employee so that he or she has a good sense of what's to come.

- Discuss the area of responsibility. Once you've shared your definition of the area, how will you invite your employee's response?
- Discuss the levels of autonomy:
  - How will you share your continuum so as to help the employee understand why you're approaching delegation in this way?
  - How will you invite the employee's response?
- Put it all together. How will you ask the employee to summarize your discussion in writing, in a way that will be helpful to both of you?
- How will you manage your self-talk? Create and write a sentence or two of believable, hopeful self-talk that will support you to fully delegate this area of responsibility.

THE SUPPORT STEP Let's assume that you've done everything as planned, and this delegation is going swimmingly. Now you just need to make sure you support your very skillful delegation conversation so as to assure a smooth transfer of power and authority in this area.

Fully supporting delegation requires three simple things:

- Honor your commitments.
- Offer feedback.
- "Move it to the right."

The first two are fairly straightforward: do what you said you were going to do, and let the employee know how he or she is doing on a regular basis. The third part is more complex and even more important. Remember that your ultimate goal is to have the employee be fully responsible for this project or area of responsibility, with only minimal involvement on your part. In order to realize that goal, both you and the employee have to work to move those elements that begin on the left end of the continuum to the right. You do this by regularly assessing the quality of the employee's work in the areas where you have less confidence and responding to improvements by offering more independence and less supervision.

If your tendency is to overdelegate (I call it the I-have-complete-faith-in-you school of delegation), be careful not to move to the right too quickly. Wait to see consistent demonstrations of the skills in question before you give more autonomy. If your tendency is to underdelegate—you are sometimes guilty of staying too involved for too long—make a concerted effort to give the person more autonomy once you see him or her getting the desired results. Remember that this person doesn't need to do it exactly the way you would; the only need is to achieve the agreed-on results.

Using this approach to delegation offers a practical way to be generous with power and authority. And it's a great example of getting by giving: as you share the responsibility for owning important work with those you lead, you free up your time to focus on being an even more effective leader.

#3 Share What They Know

One of the more frustrating habits of poor leaders is to hoard information and knowledge. About fifteen years ago, I was working with the finance executives of a very large packaged goods organization. They were in the midst of a move to a more technologically sophisticated financial management system, and we were helping them take a look at their current systems to see where the main difficulties were likely to be. In the course of our conversations, we identified one finance manager, a man who had worked for the organization all his life and was near retirement, who generated a set of fairly critical reports every month by himself. He hadn't taught anyone on his team how to do it. The only reason it came to light was that he was sick one month during the close, and there wasn't a single person, of the thousands of employees in this organization, who could fill in for him. Yikes!

This is an extreme example, but unfortunately not unique. When leaders don't share key information or knowledge, the organization becomes more fragile. If you're the only person who knows how to do an essential thing, what happens when you're not there? Not sharing critical information and knowledge makes it much harder for people to succeed individually and support the organization's success.

I've seen lots of reasons over the years for leaders not passing on what they know. Sometimes leaders feel (whether or not they would acknowledge this) that having special knowledge makes them indispensable. Sometimes they're simply unaware of the importance of people having certain information or bodies of knowledge. And sometimes (I've been guilty of this, certainly) they assume that others already know or know how to do things when they actually don't.

Why People Need to See This in Their Leaders

I've come to believe that the innate human capability we're discussing in this book—ability to assess whether someone is a good leader—arose as a tribal survival mechanism. And the aspect of generosity that focuses on sharing knowledge is a good example. Ten thousand years ago when a leader discovered a better place to spend the winter, or a quicker, more efficient way to kill a bison, or a battle cry that was more chilling to the enemy and kept that knowledge to himself, he would endanger the continued survival of the group. Sharing it, so that many people knew it and could continue to pass it on, was a powerful way to help ensure the group's survival.

Although our challenges and dangers are different today, we still want to see our leader demonstrate concern for the success and safety of the group by passing on important information and knowledge.

Generous leaders not only share information personally; they embed information sharing into the operations of the group. In larger organizations, this has come to be called "knowledge management," a fancy way of saying, "Let's make sure that the information and knowledge that is key to our success is easily available to everyone who needs it." Both individual and organizational knowledge sharing are important. Even in smaller organizations and teams, good leaders find simple, consistent ways to make sure that people are in the know on important topics.

Being Generous with Knowledge: How to Do It

The easiest way to be consistent about sharing what you know is to build it into your interactions. You can do this through reminder questions, which build your knowledge-sharing by making a habit of self-questioning at key junctures, and sharing mechanisms, which are scheduled times and places to share knowledge. Here are some examples of both:

Reminder questions

- Whenever you're about to make a key decision or take an important action, ask yourself, *Is there anyone else who needs to be involved in this?*
- Whenever there's been a mistake or problem, ask yourself, *Did I have knowledge or information that could have helped avoid this?*
- Whenever someone is new to a role or project, ask yourself, *What do I know that could make them more successful?*
- Whenever you're surprised at someone's actions, ask yourself, *What am I assuming that they know?*

You can create your own reminder questions, too, of course. These are simply some I've found most useful over the years.

Sharing Mechanisms

- Establish regular team meetings for two-way information sharing: you share critical information with your team, and they share with each other and with you.
- When you send e-mails, be sure to copy others who need the information.
- When you're working on a project with someone, establish a regular cadence of check-in calls or meetings to share essential information.
- If you find you're sharing a particular body of information or knowledge repeatedly, write it down and make it easily available to those who need it.

There's a caution here: some people err on the side of oversharing information: they give people more data, background, insight, and ideas than they can assimilate, let alone use. When you're creating the sharing mechanisms, find the middle path by making sure that you're sharing only useful and usable information with those who actually need it. For example, copying your assistant and your colleague's assistant on e-mails about a project the two of you are working on together and for which they're arranging the logistics is useful information sharing. Sending everything to your entire department, whether or not they have anything to do with the project, probably is not.

Try It: Sharing Information and Knowledge

Now you'll have a chance to translate the suggestions above into your own world:

- Write in your notebook three situations you'll be in over the next week where it would be useful to ask yourself a reminder question. Then actually do it.
- Identify two sharing mechanisms from the list above that you could institute with your team that would support you in offering and receiving critical information.

#4 Freely Give Credit, Praise, and Reward

I once worked for someone who was a miser with praise and credit. It was awful. He was a poor leader by most of the measures we're discussing, so I wasn't committed to him as my leader, but it was still awful. I once went on a sales call with him shortly after I joined the company. I made a really good connection with the client, who expressed interest in the part of the business I was newly running, a space where the company hadn't previously operated.

I was feeling pretty great until we got in the car to drive back to the office. Then my boss turned to me, frowning, and said, "It's not necessary to be so forthcoming with clients. I would have shared that information with him in time; you didn't need to share it today." I felt as if someone had stuck a pin in me; I could feel myself deflating. Fortunately, I got the opposite feedback from the client; he called me the next day and asked for more information, and I put together a proposal. We ended up doing some work for him in my area of the business. My boss never acknowledged that fact or allowed as how it might have been okay for me to let the client know about our new offer.

When leaders are chintzy with credit, praise, and reward, we feel undervalued and unappreciated. Over the years, research has shown again and again that one of the key reasons good employees leave organizations is lack of appreciation for their efforts and contributions. In other words, lack of this kind of generosity doesn't just feel bad; it's bad for business.

In contrast, another boss of mine was just the opposite. He was kind of a tough guy, not effusive or warm, but he was enormously fair and really generous. He would often tell me and others that we had done well and include the how and why. He wouldn't just say, "Great job," he'd say, "The way you wrote that report made it easy for the client to see what was important. Thanks."

In the same way, I love watching Danny Meyer interact with his employees because he seems to get such pleasure out of acknowledging their contributions. I've often heard him use one employee as a positive example to another. For instance, he will let new folks know that a particular colleague will be helpful to them in their learning, or announce that a member of the team had a useful or innovative idea that's now part of the way the company operates. People who are acknowledged in this way light up in response: they feel deeply seen and valued, and the recognition generally makes them strive to be even better.

That's the beauty of this: when you as a leader share genuine praise and give people full credit for their actions, ideas, and results, almost without exception, they are inspired to do more of the same. It feels great to be appreciated, and human nature calls us to continue to behave in ways that will garner more appreciation.

And often that's all the reward that's needed. Whenever we talk about reward to groups of leaders, they generally default to money. In fact, they'll say things like, "Sure, praise and credit are nice, but money is the real motivator." It's a common belief, but it's simply not true. In fact, there's a wonderful book, *Drive: The Surprising Truth About What Motivates Us*, in which the author, Daniel Pink, cites behavioral science showing that added money is a poor motivator, especially for highly complex and creative tasks. It's not that people don't like or want money; it's just not a great motivator of high performance. Pink notes that what is motivating to people are autonomy, mastery, and purpose: they want to have the power to direct their own lives, they want to get good at things, and they want to be involved in meaningful pursuits.

In other words, you can reward people with raises and promotions if that's possible in your organization. But don't underestimate the power of rewarding them by being generous with autonomy or flexibility, more challenging work, or more influence over decisions.

A Good Place to Start: Giving Positive Feedback

Learning to give genuine positive feedback is the simplest and probably the highest-leverage place to focus in order to improve your leadership in this area of generosity. In *Growing Great Employees*, I explore how to give both positive and corrective feedback so as to build both results and relationships. (Again, I invite you to look there for a more in-depth discussion if this is a place where you feel you need more work.) Below, I've offered a quick summary of the skill of giving positive feedback, to support your generosity in this area.

Positive feedback is a simple, powerful way to let people know that they're headed in the right direction and that you're noticing and appreciating their work. If given well and appropriately, positive feedback is extremely motivating. It also helps corrective feedback feel fair: if you regularly acknowledge your employees' contributions, they're more likely to feel you have a right to let them know when their behavior needs to be changed.

Unfortunately, not all positive feedback is equally effective. Many people give what I call "smiley face" positive feedback, like, "Great job," or, "You're the best." Although well intended, this often comes across as generic and glib, like a smiley face. Anyone can paste a smiley face on something; it requires neither thought nor attention.

What does work is specific, timely positive feedback that includes the impact—the benefit or positive effect the other person's behavior has on you, on him or her, or on the company.

Being specific is the antidote to one-size-fits-all praise and is particularly important. Giving people genuine, specific, positive feedback lets them know that you're really aware of their situation, and it tells them exactly what you'd like them to keep doing right. In other words, it not only feels personal and meaningful; it gives people the information they need to keep moving in the right direction.

Here's a simple way to cure yourself of giving smiley-face feedback. When you notice someone doing something useful or positive, take a minute to think about what exactly is good about it. Identify specific behaviors: "I really appreciated that you got this to me exactly on deadline; I know it was complex," or, "You really made our visitors feel welcome by greeting them and making sure they had what they needed," or, "You went out of your way to explain that new process to Jack." Think about how much more resonant, useful, and motivating any of those sentences would be than a generic comment like, "Nice job."

Timeliness can make your positive feedback more effective too. If you wait for months before commenting on something, people are likely to think you've got ulterior motives or wonder why you didn't say anything at the time (*Where was this when I needed it?* they think). Timely feedback is often referred to as "catching people doing something right." It's often surprising, and it's much more meaningful: you noticed it, you saw the benefit, and you took the time to comment.

Including the impact helps people see how their behavior is helpful to you, the company, or their own success. It's actually another way of being generous with knowledge: often people don't know how their actions benefit others or the organization, and when you share the impact of their actions, they understand the organization better. Explaining to them why it's important also provides them with yet another reason to keep doing it. In Daniel Pink's research about what's important to people, purpose, that is, feeling there's an important "why," is one of the big three.

When you give positive feedback, people may discount your praise out of embarrassment or learned modesty, but that's okay; you can be fairly sure they heard it and appreciated it. Making sure your feedback is specific, timely, and includes the impact are the only things you need to focus on.

One other difference between corrective and positive feedback is important. Whereas corrective feedback always needs to be given in private, positive feedback is fine to offer publicly. You might want to send around a congratulatory e-mail when a person or a team finishes a difficult project or gets excellent results or to credit someone in a meeting for work well done.

Try It: Giving Praise and Credit

You can start being more generous with praise and credit immediately.

Think of one positive thing that someone in your life (friend, spouse, coworker, employee, boss) has done in the past week or two. Write the particulars in your notebook, noting both the specifics of what it was and why it was good or useful.

Within the next twenty-four hours, share with the person, verbally or in writing, what you've written. Note both his or her reaction and how it makes you feel. (In my experience, giving positive feedback is almost as rewarding as getting it.)

#5 Provide the Resources Necessary for Others to Succeed

Doug Herzog is a collaborative and supportive leader, passionate about the idea of treating people well and making them partners in the company's success. In 2008, when Viacom, like almost every other company in America, was looking for ways to cut costs as the economy contracted, a mandate came down from the top of the company to stop paying overtime to assistants. The reasoning was that this would be an easy way to save money and operate more efficiently.

Doug knew that these first-level employees were the people in the organization who could least afford to suffer what was, in effect, a pay cut. They were young people living and working in expensive cities (New York and Los Angeles, for the most part); they were willing to work hard, and the money they got in overtime pay was often the only way they could make ends meet. He also knew that the extra time they put in was essential to the functioning of the organization. He feared that if this mandate were followed, they would most likely still be asked to work extra hours but not get paid.

After thinking about it and talking with his team, Doug decided to push back. He went to the leaders of the company and made his case. He said if they insisted, he would pay overtime out of his own bonus. They decided not to implement the no-overtime policy. And Doug, who was already seen by his folks as a generous leader, went up even further in their estimation.

Historical Necessity

The desire to have leaders who are generous with resources is also a group survival mechanism. Imagine a European village in the Middle Ages. If in lean years the lord of the manor hoards the thin harvest for himself and his family and the peasants die (or leave in search of a more generous leader), there may not be enough people left to plant, tend, and harvest the crop in the next planting season. Over a few years of the lord's miserly ways, the cycle continues, and the group dies off or disbands.

We need to know that in tough times and easy ones, our leaders will make it their business to see that we have the resources we need to survive and thrive. Because this particular aspect of generosity has historically been so core to our individual and group survival, we find its lack particularly egregious. Think of the examples both historical and current: from Marie Antoinette and her "let them eat cake" comment, Leona Helmsley and her attitude toward the "little people," the British landed gentry who let their Irish sharecroppers starve, and brutal despots like Idi Amin. When a person who's in a position of power uses that power to hoard resources to the detriment of those he or she leads, that leader becomes an object of public scorn and derision. We recount their stories over the years, decades, and centuries, saying, in effect: *Don't be like this. No one should be like this. If you lead like this, you'll come to a bad end.* (You'll remember that Marie Antoinette didn't live happily ever after.)

In day-to-day life, though, it's not usually this clear-cut. For instance, I'm pretty sure the senior executives in Doug Herzog's company weren't evil, selfish monsters; they were just shortsighted and lacked an understanding of the junior people in their organization, their lives, and how they supported the business. I'm sure they thought they were being prudent and business-like.

We're not usually dealing with issues of life and death in corporate culture, so current leaders' lack of generosity in this area is less dramatic than examples I've referenced. The kinds of resources those you lead will need in order to succeed in this day and age are things like a fair wage, the tools to do their job (technology, training, good processes, access to information), a safe and civil working environment, reasonable leave policies, and fair practices in regard to diversity.

When you're reviewing your own behavior in this regard, one simple and effective way to help ensure that you're being appropriately generous is to mentally put yourself in the other person's situation. I remember reading an article many years ago in the *Wall Street Journal* about a conservative senator who had opposed raising the minimum wage. He agreed, as a result of a wager with a liberal colleague, to try to live on the minimum wage at that time for a month. By the end of the second week, he had changed his position, becoming a firm supporter of the wage increase.

Testing Out Your Generosity
If you're wondering whether those you lead have the resources they need to succeed, the first thing to do is ask them (it's hard to put yourself in someone else's shoes without knowing what those shoes are like). Use

your listening skills to ask curiosity-based questions and restating to make sure you understand the answers. Manage your self-talk to ensure that you don't immediately dismiss any requests or concerns as unrealistic or greedy. (By the way, this is an excellent practice to engage in regularly. As a leader, it's easy to get out of touch with your employees' day-to-day jobs and their needs and constraints, and therefore fail to support them with necessary resources.)

If they do have requests for more or different resources or concerns about the resources they're now afforded, imagine you're in their situation, doing their job. Use your envisioning skills to think through what an hour or a day would be like. What would you need to be successful that they don't now have? Would you have the same requests or concerns they do?

Finally, engage' someone you believe can be truly objective about this situation—an external fair witness—who won't reflexively agree or disagree either with you or your employees. Share the situation, the employees' concerns or requests, and your point of view. Ask this person whether he or she thinks you need to provide resources you're not now providing. Then use what you've learned and understood to be realistically generous with resources and provide those things your employees need in order to be and feel successful.

Danny Meyer once said to me, "Don't you love it when people get it right and feel great about it?" *Yes,* I thought, *and they love it that you love it and that you tell them so.* It was the genuine comment of a truly generous leader.

Core Ideas

Generous leaders want their people to thrive, and they support this intention through their words and actions. When leaders are generous, their people feel cared for, seen, and valued. It creates a hopeful environment that feels rich even in hard times. People whose leaders are generous

---

become more generous in response; they are more supportive of each other, the leader, and the business.

Leaders who are *generous*:

- *Assume positive intent.* They operate on the premise that people are generally trying to do the right thing.
- *Share power and authority.* They continually find ways to give people more autonomy, influence, and responsibility.
- *Share what they know.* They provide the information and knowledge people most need and want.
- *Freely give credit, praise, and reward.* They consistently acknowledge and appreciate others' contributions.
- *Provide the resources people need to succeed.* They make sure that their people get the support they need from the organization.

EIGHT

Trustworthy

The princess held up her chained hands. "The sorcerer has the key, and he has told me that he will unlock my bonds only if a fully honest man comes to save me. Are you that man?"

"I hope so," said the young man.

Suddenly, in a flash of lightning, the sorcerer appeared, tall and skeletally thin, his skin greenish and his eyes glittering red, wrapped in a long dark cloak that gleamed and moved disturbingly.

"At last, a worthy suitor," he said, his voice deep and oddly echoing. "Are you a prince, lad?"

"No," the boy said simply.

"No?" the sorcerer raised an eyebrow. "No royal blood at all? Why on earth would I release this beautiful prize to a commoner?"

The lad looked briefly at the princess, so lovely and strong, so solemn and bright, and thought perhaps he could say he had just a bit of royal blood, if that would sway the sorcerer to his case . . .

He sighed. "No. No royal blood at all."

To the lad's astonishment, the sorcerer laughed aloud. "Good for you, boy," he said, and waved his hand.

Pat Langer is a calming presence. Partly it's because she's thoughtful and measured in her responses; partly it's because she's such a great listener.

But I'm convinced that it's primarily because she's so entirely trustworthy: in dealing with her, you feel safe and immediately relax.

The first time I met Pat, she had just been brought on as the head of human resources and legal and business affairs for Lifetime Television. I knew nothing about her or her background: all I knew was that a woman named Patricia had been hired to oversee these key staff functions.

We spent most of that first fairly brief conversation talking about the work that Proteus had been doing with Lifetime over the preceding three or four years. As I left her office, I realized two things: I had complete faith that she would respect the confidentiality of anything I had told her, and I was quite sure that she would follow through on her commitment to set up a second meeting.

Over the years, that initial sense of Pat's trustworthiness has been affirmed again and again. And it's not just my sense: when I mentioned to one of her colleagues that I was planning on using Pat as a "trustworthy exemplar" in this book, this person's response was, "Good choice. Pat's picture should be in the dictionary under the definition for the word *integrity*."

Pat is now the head of human resources for NBCUniversal, and I see the power of her trustworthiness as a leader on a daily basis. The company is in the midst of tremendous change: it was recently acquired by Comcast, in an industry that's evolving at mind-numbing speed and in a national and global economy that doesn't seem to be playing by any of the old rules. The HR function is at the heart of all this change and is itself undergoing restructuring and staff changes.

I watch Pat navigating these changes: calm, clear, entirely honest and reliable. As the months pass, I notice her impact on those around her: they're starting to trust her, and even though they may not understand why things are happening or how they're going to work out, they know that she'll tell them as much of the truth as she is able without breaching any confidences and that she'll do what she says she will do unless she simply can't. Then she'll apologize and say what she'll do instead.

It's fascinating to watch the relationships she's creating: many of the senior executives in the organization, people I've known for years, are starting to come to her for advice and counsel. They're coming not because they report to her or because they're currying political favor with her, but because she is wise and farsighted and most of all because she is trustworthy.

The Foundational Attribute

Trust is the bottom line. I believe it is the most important of the six elements. We may follow a leader who lacks farsightedness or wisdom if we sense that he or she is working to develop that attribute, but we hesitate to commit to any leader we can't trust. When we commit to leaders, we are putting our fate—at least our work fate—in their hands. We must have faith that they will do their level best to tell us the truth, follow through on their commitments, and lead us with care and skill. In the words of Stephen M. R. Covey in his wonderful book *The Speed of Trust*, we need to trust their character and their competence.

I've noted that I believe our innate ability to select for these six leadership qualities was developed in the distant past to help ensure group survival. Selecting for trustworthiness is perhaps the best example of this: in times past, choosing a leader who lied, cheated, or wasn't competent to lead—didn't have the necessary skills in war, or hunting, or governing—was a virtual death sentence. We still hold that in our collective memory, and we want to do everything possible to make sure we're following someone who won't sell us down the river, metaphorically or literally.

Trustworthiness is also the simplest element. The trustworthy leader tells the truth and keeps her word. She speaks the whole truth (sometimes omission is as much a lie as an outright misstatement) and even tells the truth about not being able to tell the truth. For example, she might say, "I can't talk about that right now because of confidentiality issues. As soon as I can speak openly, I will."

The trustworthy leader follows true speaking with true action: he does what he says he's going to do. In the rare instance when he is unable to keep his word, he apologizes as soon as possible and lets people know what he's going to do to rectify the situation. He doesn't tell people what they want to hear; he tells them what he believes to be true and what he actually intends to do and is capable of doing.

People also look to trustworthy leaders to act in ways that will benefit the enterprise. If I observe that a leader behaves in ways that advance him personally at the expense of larger goals, it's hard, if not impossible, to believe that leader won't choose to throw me and my colleagues under any passing bus if it will serve his own success.

Finally, trustworthy leaders are competent. They demonstrate the capability to do the job they have been given (and are honest about any deficits in that regard and how they'll go about addressing them), and they get the results they've committed to achieving.

When There's No Trust

Untrustworthy leaders are simply not leaders in the eyes of their followers. I've seen it time and again over the years: an untrusted leader is just "the boss." People will do what they must to keep their jobs, and they may find other leaders in the organization to whom they can commit and in whom they can put their trust. But their relationship with the untrustworthy leader will be characterized by self-protection and avoidance. They will share as little as possible of their real thoughts and concerns and redirect their passion and enthusiasm for pursuits outside work. The best people will tend to leave over time, consciously or unconsciously looking for leaders in whom they can place their trust—leaders it feels safe to follow. And the lack of individual trust shows up organizationally in profound and negative ways: untrustworthy leaders most often preside over cultures filled with time-wasting political intrigue, grudging and mediocre customer care, and less-than-stellar business results.

How to Get an Engaged, Committed Team

Be trustworthy. Trustworthiness inspires loyalty and makes us feel safe. We relax and let go of the need to protect ourselves and monitor our reactions. We can bring more of who we are to work: creativity, hopefulness, and honesty. When a leader is worthy of trust, people reward him or her by becoming more trustworthy themselves. Trust is the essential bond between a true leader and her followers.

How to Be Trustworthy

You may have been reading these paragraphs thinking, *Yes, that's true, I've seen it and felt it. I am my best self when I've worked for trustworthy leaders, and that's the sort of leader I want to be.* Or you may have had exactly the opposite reaction. You may be thinking: *That's bullshit. Business isn't about trust; it's about winning. Successful CEOs care only about the bottom line.* You are welcome, of course, to think what you like. And if you really believe that, you'll probably find the rest of this chapter a waste of your time.

However, I have to disagree with you. Over the thirty years I've been working with leaders of all kinds, I've met hundreds of deeply trustworthy, ethical, high-integrity leaders, and I've seen the kinds of organizations they create and the results they get. I've seen the impact they have on the people around them and the world they live in. Based on my observation, I believe that being and having trustworthy leaders is a practical necessity in this complex and fragile world. I invite you to explore the possibility of becoming a trusting and trustworthy leader.

Leaders Who Are Trustworthy

1. Tell the truth as they understand it
2. Do what they say they will do
3. Keep confidences

4. Speak and act for the greater good
5. Are capable and get results

As with generosity, it's especially important to use your fair witness skills as you assess yourself in this attribute. Most of us want to think we're trustworthy, and most of us believe we are.

In fact, you might even want to get some third-party fair witnessing on this one. Choose someone who knows you well in a work setting and is willing to tell you what he or she sees, with a supportive intention but without pulling any punches. Ask this colleague to read each of the five statements above and tell you how consistently they see you behaving in these ways: inconsistently (growth area), consistently (strength), or nearly always, and in a way that provides an example for others (key strength).

Once you have an accurate sense of your demonstrated trustworthiness, focus particularly on the elements below where you and your fair witness feel you're least consistent.

#1 Tell the Truth as They Understand It

I've only "fired" a handful of clients in my life as a consultant. Once or twice it was because they saw the world and people's motivations so profoundly differently than I do that I couldn't imagine how we could be helpful to them. Every other time, it's been a matter of trust. One instance stands out in particular. This happened almost fifteen years ago when I was first developing this model. I was talking with the CEO of a small entertainment company about the possibility of having me coach one of his executives. He seemed reasonably clear about this woman's strengths and weaknesses, and the conversation was going fairly well. I was explaining to him the precoaching process we use, where we interview six to eight people who work closely with the coachee to get a sense of how this person is perceived and so that we can share that perception with him or her. We hold the specific remarks in confidence; the coachee gets a summary report that focuses on key strengths and weaknesses noted by the majority of the interviewees.

The CEO said, "Well, you can tell her you're going to talk to people, but I only want you to talk to me, and I want you to write the report based on what I say." I was speechless for a few moments, and my face must have reflected my shock.

"Here's the deal," he went on. "She's pretty good, but she's not as good as she thinks she is, and other people will just confuse the issue. I want this report to take her down a peg."

It was untrustworthy on so many levels, I couldn't even begin to respond. More important, I didn't want to. I told him I didn't think our approach would be a good fit for him and got out of there as quickly as possible. I felt slightly grubby for the rest of the day.

This is a particularly egregious example of not telling the truth, but milder versions of it are fairly common in business. When leaders behave like this in one situation—manipulating the facts toward whatever outcome they want versus telling the truth—we immediately assume that they do it in other situations too. Once we believe we can't trust what leaders say, we tell them as little as possible, and cover ourselves as extensively as we can, so that we feel protected from their lying and manipulation. It's not a good prescription for a high-performance workplace.

Even Little Lies Are Lies

For most of us, our non-truth-telling is less black-and-white than the example I just gave and less manipulative. We tell one person that we're going to pursue his idea, and then tell the next person, with a completely different idea, that her idea is great and that we're going to pursue it. Even when we know we can't do both things or that the ideas are in fact contradictory, we tell ourselves it's okay to act this way. Maybe we weren't sure which way to go, or don't want to disappoint either employee, or don't want to cut off our options prematurely. Unfortunately, when we finally decide which way to go, the person whose idea we're not using feels lied to.

In another common leadership situation, person A comes into our office to complain about person B. We more or less agree: "Yeah, that person definitely tends to get a little carried away; it's irritating." But then, when person B comes in to complain, in turn, about person A, we agree with this person's assessment too: "Yeah, I know he's hard to read and can be a stick in the mud. It gets in the way of progress." We might think we're just being understanding or keeping the peace. But if the two people compare notes, they'll come to the conclusion that you're saying things you don't really believe to one of them (or perhaps both).

All Lies Are Visible

Sometimes we can convince ourselves that these untruths, half-truths, or misstatements will somehow be invisible. Maybe people won't notice or won't check in with each other. It's simply not true. As a friend used to say, "You know we can see you, right?" When you're the leader, people are generally hyperaware of your behavior. They want to know whether it will be safe and productive to follow you, and they're especially looking for signs of your trustworthiness (or the lack thereof). Assume that if you shade the truth, misrepresent some checkable fact, or say one thing to one person, and something different to someone else, it will be seen, commented on, and judged.

Cultivating Honesty

To make sure that you are demonstrating this aspect of trustworthiness— that you're consistently telling the truth as you understand it—start by getting a clear sense of whether you have a problem in this area. Think about feedback you've gotten at work and from friends or family. People generally won't come right out and say they don't think you're trustworthy. However, they might say things like, "Sometimes I'm not sure if you're telling me the whole story," or, "You seem to change your mind a lot," or, "I get the feeling sometimes you just go along to keep the peace." These and other statements like them are all well-meaning, diplomatic code for, "I don't trust what you say." If you've heard this from others, I'd suggest you take a closer look at how you operate in this realm.

The next step, and this requires a good deal of fair witnessing, is to catch yourself. Next time you're in a situation and are tempted to be less than honest (telling someone a spun version of events to make yourself look better; giving one person a different account of something than you've told someone else to avoid a conflict or get out of a jam; saying something behind someone's back that you wouldn't say to his or her face), simply stop talking.

Now take a deep breath. If you need some time to reflect and decide how to tell the truth, ask to continue the conversation later. If you decide not to say anything more on the topic (sometimes silence really is golden), either change the subject or say something neutral like, "That's interesting," or, "I don't really have anything to add." Or simply state the facts with no spin.

I predict that the more you make the effort to become aware of your behavior in this area, the more you'll be surprised at (and perhaps appalled by) how often you play with the facts. What makes this area particularly difficult is that there *are* some situations where it's okay to tell a sanitized version of the truth. If your five year old's first attempt at drawing the family dog looks more like a Rorschach test, it's okay to say, "Oh, I see, sure, there's his eye and that's his ear . . . " If your husband notes that his old pants are "a little tight" and you are a kind person, you simply smile and agree. And because we know that these little white lies are okay and even positive at times, we tend to give ourselves way too much latitude, convincing ourselves that we're telling harmless white lies when in truth we're revising the truth to our own advantage or to avoid a difficult but necessary conversation.

One question I've found helpful in holding myself to a high but reasonable standard of truthfulness is, *Who does this benefit?* If I can honestly say that I'm omitting a truth or telling the truth in a more dip-lomatic way to benefit another person—save them from unnecessary embarrassment or help them stay focused or motivated, for instance—it's probably okay. However, if I'm being less than honest in order to benefit myself—to make myself look better; to avoid the consequences of my actions; because I'm lacking in courage; or to win at another's expense—it's probably not okay; I'm being untrustworthy.

Try It: Telling the Truth

Now you'll have a chance to review a recent conversation where you were less than honest and decide how you'd do it over. Then you'll focus on creating a simple way to catch yourself going forward.

Think of a conversation you've had within the past few weeks where you shaded the truth for your own benefit. You can write the particulars in your notebook to get clearer about what happened and why you said what you did. Be brutally honest with yourself.

If you had this conversation to do over right now, how would you change what you did or said? Note the changes you'd make in your notebook.

See if you can isolate the moment in that conversation when you could have chosen to behave in this more trustworthy way.

Think about and write in your notebook how you can catch yourself and choose to be more honest in similar choice point moments going forward.

#2 Do What They Say They Will Do

Pat Langer is nearly flawless in this regard. In all my interactions with her over the years, she either does what she says she's going to do (this happens in the vast majority of cases), or she lets me know why she's not going to be able to fulfill her commitment and tells me, or creates with me, an alternative plan.

We find it liberating to deal with someone whose word is their bond: it frees up all our energy to focus on the important elements in the relationship and on the work we're doing together. In contrast, when someone doesn't keep his or her word, it's like sitting on a chair you think might break: you never put your full weight on it, and you always have your eye out for a sturdier chair to sit on. It's exhausting.

Recently Pat got some feedback about her style as a leader. Not surprisingly, people saw her as being trustworthy, open, and discreet. They also said they wanted to have more interaction with her. Again, I wasn't surprised. She's a "strong chair," and it feels good and safe to them to deal with her, especially given that her organization is undergoing a great deal of change.

Keeping your word is especially important in changing times. In times of high change and ambiguity, people need even more consistent demonstrations that they can rely on their leaders' promises. Over the past couple of years, I've observed some leaders casually changing direction or commitments without explanation and often without clarifying the new direction. I've also seen the havoc it can wreak on their organizations. It's not only the emotional havoc of people feeling unsure, blindsided, lied to, and disrespected. It's functional havoc as well: people being unclear about how to proceed, working at cross purposes, or stuck, unwilling to let go of the original direction without a clear new mandate.

Changing Course Well

Changing times makes it harder than ever to keep your word. Even leaders who try their hardest to do what they say they'll do often find that circumstances beyond their control require them to rethink and change direction. And when that happens, it's critical to be as trustworthy in making the change as in making the initial promise.

Pat recently found that she was going to have to approach a restructuring issue differently than she had anticipated and differently than she had communicated to some of her people. What made it even more complicated was that the redirection had come from her superiors and reflected an approach with which she wasn't entirely comfortable. She thought deeply about how to communicate the change to her team, and it was a beautiful thing to see: she told them that they would need to think in a new way about how to address the situation, and she let them know that the change was a result of a new direction she had gotten from her superiors. She also let them know that though she wasn't entirely in agreement with the direction, she understood her bosses' point of view and was committed to working with the team to find a solution that would work for them, the team, and the organization.

One thing I noticed: if Pat's bosses had been in the room when she was offering this explanation, they would have been fine with what they were hearing. She didn't break trust with them in the process. This is an important element of this aspect of trustworthiness: when you need to change direction, it's not okay to take the easy (and less trustworthy) road of throwing someone else under the bus as a rationale for the change.

Think Before You Don't Act

Finally, one way to support yourself in keeping your commitments is to think consciously about the impact of not fulfilling a commitment, especially without communicating the change. Before you let a commitment slip, think through who it will affect and to what degree. I still remember something that happened to me almost twenty-five years ago that demonstrated the importance of this leader behavior to me: my boss at the time had asked me to work on a project that he told me was very important to the business—a high priority. He said that once I'd finished my part of the work, he would review the results, revise it with me, and then share it with the whole organization. I spent many hours over the next few weeks, outside of my regular workday, gathering the information he needed and framing it in a way I thought was both compelling and simple. When I brought it to him, he looked surprised. "Oh, didn't I tell you?" he said. "We decided to go in another direction." He wouldn't even let me hand it to him.

No further explanation was forthcoming. Not only was I disappointed and angry; I stopped putting my faith in his commitments from that moment forward. The next time he asked me to do something, I spent quite a bit of time checking along the way with him and others to see if it was still happening. I began to notice that others also operated in this way, and it helped me understand a lot of the inefficiencies and rework I was seeing in the organization. It obviously had a big emotional impact on me: I'm still telling this story as a cautionary tale all these years later.

Try It: Keeping Your Word, Even When It Changes

Think of the last time you didn't do something you said you'd do. It could be something as minor as not returning a call when promised or as significant as missing an important deadline. Write down the specifics: what you promised and what got in the way. Then consider what you could have done differently to keep this commitment.

If circumstances truly beyond your control kept you from keeping your word, what could you have done to say what happened and what you'll do instead? Perhaps you could text the person you promised to call, letting him or her know you're running late and asking to reschedule. Or you could alert your team as soon as possible about what's affecting the deadline and suggest a quick call to replan.

Once you get in the habit of keeping your commitments and change them only when necessary and in a clear and honorable way, you'll notice that people react to you differently: they're more likely to keep their promises to you and to "say why and what they'll do differently" when they don't. When you set a high bar of trustworthiness in this way, most people respond in kind.

#3 Keep Confidences

David Seltzer is another trustworthy leader for whom I have great respect. David is the managing partner of Management 360, an artist and literary management company based in Los Angeles. In an industry often characterized by questionable dealings, loose lips, and a pronounced lack of ethics, the folks at Management 360 have made integrity one of their key competitive advantages. David is extraordinarily discreet; I've known and worked with him for a number of years, and he has never once revealed to me a single piece of information about any of his celebrity clients. He doesn't even drop seemingly harmless pieces of information about who he's traveling to support or meet with, information that could make him look cool but might possibly compromise his clients' privacy.

He has high standards of discretion internally, too. When a colleague tells him something in confidence, it stays confidential. I've noticed how his colleagues, most of whom have worked with him for many years, rely on his discretion; they share sensitive topics with him without hesitation and feel safe to do so.

As with the first two elements of trustworthiness, when leaders keep confidences, they create an atmosphere of safety and calm. People are more likely to focus on doing the work as opposed to figuring out how to protect themselves from the leader's indiscretion.

I've also seen the opposite. A leader I've been coaching recently is a very open person; unfortunately, she is sometimes as open with others' personal information as she is with her own. When I began working with her, one of the things she worried about was that her folks had stopped speaking up; she couldn't get them to share their point of view with her. She felt that they were being evasive, especially when she asked them to note whether they disagreed with others' perspectives. I noted the feedback she had gotten about not keeping personal information confidential and told her I thought this was why people weren't being straightforward. "I get that," she said, "and I'll be much more careful in the future. But that's personal stuff; I'm asking for their opinions on business issues." I explained to her that people don't make that distinction in their heads. Once they see someone as not keeping confidences, they're loath to share any potentially sensitive or controversial information with you: they simply don't trust that it's safe. It was a rude awakening: she realized that she had a good deal of work to do to rebuild that trust.

Just Don't Say It

This is a simple thing to do; I'm not even going to propose an activity for you to try. But simple doesn't mean easy, and if you're used to playing fast and loose with confidential information, this can be a tough habit to change. So I'll offer you a self-talk mantra to use in support of keeping confidences. In all situations where you're about to share something someone else has told you, ask yourself first, *How would I feel if that person were hearing me say this?* Asking that question mentally has stopped me in my verbal tracks many, many times, and I hope it does the same for you.

#4 Speak and Act for the Greater Good

Speaking and acting for the greater good goes to the heart of your role as a leader. People need to see that their leaders not only speak for the group and its goals, but act in accordance with their pronouncements. Human survival throughout history has depended on having leaders who speak for the group and then follow it up with action. If a leader supports the group's success verbally but acts in ways that don't line up with those words, it's like a flashing red light telling us not to put our fate in his or her hands.

Centuries ago that might have meant a chieftain telling us that if we'd fight under him, he'd protect us from the invaders, and then surreptitiously moving his own family and possessions, and even himself, out of danger. Today's version of that is the CEO who assures his people that he won't do mass layoffs, while the scuttlebutt from the grapevine is that there are already secret meetings about which heads will roll and when.

Again, remember that *people can see you.* And they're looking hard at this particular thing. If there's a dissonance between your words and your deeds in support of the organization or the team, they will withdraw their support from you, and quickly. In fact, history is littered with the bones of leaders who purported to be the supporters and protectors of their people but were not.

Back It Up

One way to avoid stumbling in this area is not to make promises you can't keep on behalf of the organization. David Seltzer is very good at this. Over the past few years, I've been supporting him and his partners to create a clear vision and strategy for the future of the organization. Recently he and I have been talking about putting together a town hall meeting to share the outcomes of the session with the rest of the organization and include them more fully in the process. David's main concern is ensuring that the senior team shares only the goals and commitments that they can keep. He sees the benefit of the partners saying in public what they'll do to support the organization's success, but he's clear that if they tell everyone that the partner group will do certain things and those things don't happen, that will be seen as a powerful negative instance of the partners not acting in support of the organization.

Fortunately, all his partners share this concern. I suspect that in the session before the town hall meeting, we'll spend time making sure they believe they can back up their words with action in support of the organization.

In contrast, I've known leaders who speak in glowing terms about the future, thinking to inspire people, but then they don't back it up in their day-to-day actions by doing the things it will take to get there. I suspect you've seen the effect of this. Most of us have. What does it feel like when a leader paints a positive picture of what will happen for the team or the company and then doesn't follow through? Even though he or she may be well intended, it still feels like a bait-and-switch. You feel lied to, and you're much less likely to believe this person the next time.

Be Tough in Support of the Larger Goal

Often "backing it up" requires doing and saying difficult things. This is closely related to doing things that are the personally uncomfortable part of courageous. David is also great at this. A couple of years ago, I recommended one of our consultants to support Management 360 in an organizational development project they were considering. David had had a few interactions with this person, and didn't feel he was a fit for them. Although I'm sure it was not the most pleasant conversation for him, David shared his point of view and let me know they didn't want to involve my colleague in the project. He could easily have gone along with my recommendation, even though he didn't think it was best for him and his partners—or not used him and told me some made-up story about why, which would have been a whole different kind of untrustworthy.

One great public example of this was when Steve Jobs came back to Apple in 1997. He made a lot of changes that were deeply uncomfortable for people because he truly felt they were best for the organization. He said what he thought needed to change and why, and then he acted on it. From what I understand, Jobs was at times a difficult person, but those who worked for and with him always felt he was doing his best to act for the organization's success.

Try It: Aligning Words and Actions

Let's practice with a situation that's confronting you right now:

- What's one thing you feel strongly that your group needs to do differently in order to be a more effective team or to get better results? Focus on something you've not yet spoken about to the group.
- Think about and write down in your notebook how you'll speak to the team about this issue—for example:

> We need to address issues directly with each other. When we have a problem with someone else on the team, we tend either to go to another colleague and complain or tattle on the person to his or her boss.
> I really want each of us, me included, to speak directly to the person we're having an issue with. I know that can be daunting, but if we don't do it, we'll lose trust in each other, and our issues won't get resolved.

- Review what you've written. What will you need to do in order to make sure your actions line up with your words? How will you personally support this change?

#5 Are Capable and Get Results

In *The Speed of Trust,* Stephen M. R. Covey notes that when we trust others, it's a result of trusting both their character and their competence. I agree wholeheartedly. The first four elements of trustworthy go to character, and this last element goes to competence.

Even in the fairy tales that provide the map of these leader attributes, the boy not only has to be honest and discreet, and to speak and act in service of the greater good, he has to (in the words of my dear husband) "get 'er done." There are tasks to be accomplished on the way to saving the princess, and he has to be (or become) capable of doing them in order to get the necessary results.

All of the leaders I've profiled throughout the book exemplify this element: they are highly capable, and they get the results they're held accountable for achieving. This is the most skill based of all the elements. It's important that you have the core skills and experience needed for the position you're in so that you can get the results required. I've met too many leaders over the years who demonstrated most or all of the other attributes but were ill suited for their job through either lack of experience or deficit of skills, and as a result, they failed as leaders. Think of it this way: being able to do the job is the price of admission.

Increasing Your Capability

The good news is that it's relatively easy to acquire job skills and experience, that is, to become more capable. In our leadership and management training and coaching, I see people improving their skills every day. In fact, one of the great joys of my professional life is watching those whom I support grow over the years: folks who started out in entry-level jobs gradually gaining skills and experience and succeeding in increasingly demanding and broader jobs. And (more good news) you can use your other leader attributes to help you develop your job skills:

- Being *farsighted* can help you get a clear sense of your own hoped-for career future, so you can build a plan for adding career skills and experiences to get there.

- Being *passionate* about your own success can keep you committed to improving your skills.
- Being *courageous* can support you in learning those things that may be awkward or uncomfortable for you and in asking for others' help.
- Being *wise* can help you to see your own strengths and weaknesses clearly and learn from your mistakes.
- Being *generous* will mean you share your insights and skills with others, one of the best ways to deepen your own understanding.

In the final chapter, I'll help you make an overall plan for developing in the leader attributes, and if this is an area of development for you, you can plan how to approach it.

Results

Fortunately, you've just learned one of the keys to being seen as capable and results oriented: make only promises you can keep. I notice that the leaders who consistently get results are clear-eyed and realistic about the results they can get (fair witness). They sign up for only the results they believe are achievable. In fact, this is really another aspect of doing what you say you'll do.

Courage comes into this at times as well. If your boss is requiring you to get results that you don't believe are possible, you need to say so. And then your wisdom comes into play: you need to make a case for why you think it's not possible, based on your experience and information. Finally, you continue to be trustworthy and say what you'll do instead.

You may have noticed that I've started to address all six attributes as I close this chapter. That's because I want you now to put them back together and think of them not as separate things but as six aspects of a single powerful entity: the leader people want to follow.

Core Ideas

Trustworthy leaders create an environment of safety and calm, where people feel they can put down roots and grow. They relax into the work and the team rather than guarding their words and actions. When people trust their leader, much more of their energy is available to the organization, and conversation becomes easier and more open. A trusting environment supports simplicity, efficiency, and innovation.

Leaders who are *trustworthy*:

- *Tell the truth as they understand it.* They don't shade or position the truth to benefit themselves: they are honest.

- *Do what they say they will do.* They keep their commitments. When they can't, they're clear and honest about what's changed.

- *Keep confidences.* They're rigorous about discretion; if they say they'll keep something private, they will.

- *Speak and act for the greater good.* Their words and actions are consonant and support the success of the enterprise.

- *Are capable and get results.* They have the skills and experience to do the job before them, and they do it.

NINE

Friends for the Journey

The king and queen agreed at once. The princess and the youngest brother were married. The father, the much-chastened brothers, the little men, and even the faery-woman came to the wedding and celebrated his good fortune. The princess and the lad were glad together, and when the old king and queen died after long and happy lives, the princess and the youngest-brother-turned king ruled with kindness, justice, and joy.

As I was reading fairy tales to my children all those years ago, I noticed that the hero of the story always had help along the way. I believe this is another important instruction about how to become a worthy leader. It seems to me the message being communicated here is this: you cannot do this on your own; leading is a group endeavor. Leadership is about the survival of the whole. Being an effective leader not only requires the support *of* others; it requires support *from* others.

And just as with the six leader attributes, I found a pattern. In most of the leader stories I read, three key types of supporters appear to aid the leader-in-training: there's almost always someone with magical powers or unusual insight, almost always someone who believes in the boy even when others don't, and almost always someone (or someones) who appears along the way and just happens to have a skill or resource critical to the boy's success. I call these three different types of helpers *wizards*, *well-wishers*, and *wild cards*. Each appears and offers support in response to the boy's demonstration of one or more of the attributes, and they support him along the way to demonstrate or develop the other attributes so that he can complete his quest and become a true leader.

The wizard in our story at the start of this book is the faery-woman. She gives the boy important insights that help him to avoid failure, and she offers to help him again when he truly needs her aid. The boy remembers her counsel at a critical juncture, and it keeps him moving safely toward his destiny.

The well-wisher is the boy's father. He doesn't push the boy into the quest but lets him make his own decision and affirms his highest intentions. He supports the boy's journey, even when resources are scarce and even when others can't see the boy's potential.

The wild cards are the little men. They seem like a danger or a possible impediment at first, but the boy wins them over with his farsightedness and courage, and they're later revealed to have the one thing (the magical dart gun) that he can use to overcome the essential obstacle to his quest.

And, as you might suspect, having stayed with me thus far, I'm now going to help you translate this into the twenty-first century and your own leader journey.

Finding a Wizard

Sadly for us, our wizards aren't generally waiting conveniently by the nearest well, asking us to share our bread or coins. So how do you recognize them and take advantage of their help? I've noticed that in the stories, wizards mostly reveal themselves in response to the hero's demonstration of generosity. I believe the message here is to be generous to others, and useful people will show up and be generous to you. I've found that to be true in modern workplace wizardry. I notice, for instance, that Danny Meyer, one of my exemplars of generosity, seems to be a magnet for good wizards who want to support his success by offering useful insights and processes. For example, Richard Goldberg is one person who's been extraordinarily useful to Danny's organization over the years; he's a deeply thoughtful and accomplished business adviser and lawyer, a tribal elder with enormous experience helping businesses succeed. Danny uses Richard consistently as a wizard, benefiting from his general insight and his specific counsel.

So the first way to find a wizard is to be a generous leader. Wizards are attracted to offer their wizardly help to those who help others.

Let's say you're being generous. Now, how do you recognize a wizard when he or she shows up? Or, alternatively, how do you go about looking for them? Here are the key characteristics of the wizards who can support you in becoming a leader that others want to follow:

- They see you clearly and tell you what they see.
- They want to help you if they believe your cause is worthy and you have the potential to be a good leader.
- They have insights into your challenges and can offer possible solutions.
- They have "magic": approaches, processes, templates, or learning that can help you become a better leader.

At the risk of sounding self-aggrandizing, I know what wizards look and act like because I am one. In fact, all of the consultants at Proteus are wizards. We do precisely the things I've listed above. So one place to look for wizards is outside your organization in the form of coaches or consultants whose services you can engage. Be careful, though: there are lots of coaches and consultants floating around, and not all of them have real wizard powers (I'm going to wring everything I can from this metaphor). If you're thinking about working with an outside person to support your leadership development, make sure to vet him or her. In your interactions with your potential wizard or wizards, put on your fair witness hat and make sure they demonstrate (not just say they demonstrate, but actually do it) the four attributes above.

As an example, I'll use someone whose wizard powers I have observed for many years: my business partner, Jeff Mitchell. Jeff is a wonderful wizard for a client of ours who is a senior executive in human resources for a large retail organization. He sees both her strengths and her weaknesses clearly, and he shares that perspective with her in a way that's designed both to help her grow and help her avoid pitfalls along the way. I also know, based on conversations we've had, that he believes her cause is worthy and that she can be a good leader. He trusts that she's a smart, well-intentioned person who wants to do good work and is working for a positive, successful, and reasonably well-run organization. And he believes she has both the desire and the capability to be the kind of leader people want to follow, the kind of leader I've described for you in this book. He sees both the organization and her role in it quite clearly, and he's aware of the challenges that face her. He offers insights into the nature of those challenges and ideas about how to resolve them. His "magic" is the Proteus models and approaches—the tools he brings to his work with her and her team that help them get ready and stay ready for their future by envisioning the future more clearly, operating together more effectively, achieving their goals, and helping themselves and others become more followable leaders.

Wizards don't have to come from outside your organization, though. For instance, Jeff is also a wizard to me in many of the ways I've referenced above. Some of the best wizards are those we call mentors. If you're looking to find a mentor/wizard, listen to the chatter in your organization about the senior people. When you hear about someone who seems to demonstrate the four qualities I've described, go to that person and ask if he or she will mentor you. Again, generosity helps: if there's something you can offer to do in return, making that offer will demonstrate your understanding and respect for the fact that you're asking something of this wizard. For instance, a young woman I met recently who wanted to get more comfortable sharing her ideas with senior people (she was working on her farsightedness) went to an executive in her organization for whom she had a lot of respect and asked if he could help her in this area. She offered in return to work on a digital project he was leading because it was in an area of technology she knew well. He agreed, and she recently e-mailed me to say that their time together had already been enormously helpful to her.

Most important, when you find a good wizard, either inside or outside the organization, be very careful to value this person's contributions. Many a fairy-tale hero has lost the support of his wizard by not appreciating the wisdom or making the best use of the magic he or she shares. The best way to value what wizards offer is to take proper advantage of it: to follow through on their wise suggestions and use their "magic" for good. The second important way is to thank them and let them know how they're helping.

Well-Wishers Are Your Haven

In our story, the boy's father was purely supportive of him. You just know that if all the merchants in their village were sitting around talking about their kids and somebody turned to him and said, "So what about that youngest son of yours? What's his deal? Is he a little slow or something?" The father would have said something like, "Oh no, he's a great kid. Really helps me out around the cottage; puts up with his brothers, who can be a handful. Honest as the day is long. He's just quiet. But if you get him talking, he has smart things to say." In other words, well-wishers support you unconditionally. It's not that they don't see your weaknesses; rather, they focus first on your strengths and potential and are always there to support your success.

Well-wishers support your highest intentions. They don't collude with your me-against-the-world complaints. If you're trying to blame your problems on somebody else, they'll empathize, but they won't let you off the hook. They call you out to be your best self. Here are the key characteristics of well-wishers:

- They see and acknowledge your strengths and potential.
- They inspire and help you to be your best.

- They support you in word and deed in your efforts to succeed.
- They accept and celebrate you as you are.

It's wonderful if you can find a well-wisher at work. The very best managers and leaders are well-wishers. If you have the opportunity to work for one, it could be the best experience of your professional life.

It's more common to find well-wishers at home. I am extraordinarily fortunate in that my husband, Patrick, is my deepest well-wisher. One thing I'm learning by having him in my life is that a true and unwavering well-wisher offers a powerful foundation for your efforts to be the kind of leader and the kind of person you want to be. Because he sees and celebrates the best in me on a daily basis, I feel strengthened and freed to keep growing and expanding, to find out what and who I'm truly capable of being.

And that's the power of well-wishers. If you're serious about developing yourself as a true leader, it can be a somewhat daunting endeavor. It's essential to have someone (or, ideally, more than one someone) who believes in your potential and is committed to helping you succeed.

Look around. You may already have one or more well-wishers in your life. If not, I'll offer this advice: the best way to have well-wishers is to be one. Review that list above. Are you that person for other people in your life: your spouse, children, employees, friends? Cultivate your own well-wisherness, and I suspect you'll begin to get it in return.

Wild Cards Are Just That

I call them wild cards for a reason. In poker, a wild card can have any value, and it's hard to know how it will help until you see the hand you're dealt. In fact, you sometimes don't even know whether a wild card will help at all until you know the situation you're in.

Think about the little men in our story. At first, our hero wasn't sure whether they were going to help him out or eat him for dinner. I notice that this is also true of modern wild cards. Think about that wacky guy down the hall whom everybody thinks is probably kind of brilliant but has a reputation for being the biggest curmudgeon or the flakiest dreamer in the organization. He may in fact be the only person who has the one quirky skill set you need to finish a stalled project or who just happens to be college buddies with the head of information technology and can explain to him what your department needs in a way that would actually work. When you first start talking to him, you're not sure if he's going to order you out of his office or solve all your problems.

With wild cards, you never know. There's no list of characteristics for wild cards and just one critical attribute: they're people who have something you really need in your quest, and you don't know that until they're on your side.

So how do you get them on your side? You may recall that the way the boy in our story tipped the scales with the little men, toward support and away from dinner, was to be farsighted. He told them about his quest, and why it was important, in a compelling and inclusive way, and they were inspired to join him.

It's the same with modern wild cards. If you are consistently farsighted—see possible positive futures, articulate that in a compelling and inclusive way, model your vision, see past obstacles, and invite others to participate—then among the people who are attracted and inspired by your far-sightedness, there will be some wild cards. And then you'll have to be generous and assume positive intent in order to see past whatever strangeness they may carry along with their gifts. You'll also have to be courageous to take advantage of their help. As with the boy and the little men, what they bring to you quite often requires you to step out of your comfort zone.

Here's a great wild card example. About ten years ago, I was working with a woman named Ellen who had just been promoted to senior vice president of sales in her company. She was assessing all the folks in her function as to whether they were "in the right seats on the right bus," in the words of Jim Collins. There was one guy who she had pretty much decided to fire based on her first few interactions with him (she was a very quick decision maker, which was both a strength and a weakness). When I asked her why, she said, "He's just not the kind of guy I want in sales. He's too quiet and hard to read, he gets tongue-tied if I ask him a direct question, and I can't imagine he's going to bring much to the table." I told her that I had actually heard some very good things about him from his colleagues and encouraged her to take a little time to find out more about him before deciding. She agreed that was probably wise (though I could tell she thought I was wrong).

A couple of weeks later, she held an off-site meeting for her whole team, where she outlined her vision for sales for the next couple of years. One of the main elements she focused on was the idea of expanding into the Hispanic market. It was a segment of the population hugely underserved by their industry and with whom their brand really resonated, but they hadn't taken advantage of that fact. I was facilitating the meeting, and as she spoke, I noticed that the man she had questions about sat up and leaned forward, looking very excited, for him (he really was a quiet, hard-to-read guy). When she was done, he started speaking immediately. "Ellen, I did the research on that, and I completely agree with what you're saying. In fact, I have a lot of professional and personal connections in the Latin community—my wife's Colombian—and I'd really like to help figure out how to make this happen."

Voilà: wild card.

Try It: Finding Your Friends

To identify at least one of each type of supporter for your leadership journey and decide how to enlist them in your quest, begin by noting those you already have:

- Who are your wizards?
- Who are your well-wishers?
- Who are your wild cards?

If you're fortunate enough to have all three already, congratulations. Treat them like the gold and jewels they are, and keep your eyes open for others. If you're missing one or more, use the approach below to help find them.

Wizards

Think about people already in your circle who could be wizards for you. Write their names in your notebook under "possible wizards."

Check to see if they have the wizard characteristics. Pick out the one you think most demonstrates the characteristics and who you think would be open to wizarding for you. Circle his or her name.

Now decide how to be generous in inviting him or her to be your wizard. How will you ask, and what will you offer?

Well-Wishers

First, review the characteristics of well-wishers and note the people in your life toward whom *you* most behave in that way. In other words, for whom are *you* a well-wisher? Write their names in your notebook.

Could any of those people be well-wishers for you, especially if you were more consistent in being a well-wisher for them? If yes, circle their names, and decide how you'll be more fully supportive of them. If no, I suggest you do some wise reflecting on the nature of your relationships. If there's no one in your circle who is or could be a well-wisher, even if you are a well-wisher for them, you might want to think deeply about the quality of your current relationships.

Wild Cards

Think of a time when you happened on a wild card, saw the value, and took advantage of this person's offer. What did you do that allowed that to happen? Think about and write down some ways you can more consistently use those approaches with new people in order not to overlook their possible wild-cardness—for example, "I questioned my initial negative assumptions," or, "I got curious about what they might bring to the party."

And now, let's put it all together: your plan for becoming the worthy leader, the leader whom others want to follow.

TEN

Your Own Tale

Once upon a time . . .

In the story I've used throughout this book, it all just happened to fall into place: the boy, his brothers, the quest, his supporters, the tests of his leader attributes. That's the nature of fairy tales: they are freed from the constraints of reality, so that they can show us the perfect example as a model.

We, however, have to create our own story from the materials that reality presents to us. It's more like a scavenger hunt than a fairy tale. Given that, I thought it would be useful to give you a little guidance here for pulling it all together to make a practical simple plan for your development as a followable leader.

Reassess Your Current State

Go back to the page in Chapter Two where I asked you to do an initial self-assessment in the six leader attributes. Pull out your notebook here as well to reflect on all you've thought about and learned. Now that you know a good deal more about each of the attributes, including the key behaviors for demonstrating them, I encourage you to reassess your current state as a followable leader. Look at how you initially rated yourself in each attribute (growth area, strength, or key strength). It might

also help to look back at the pages in Chapters Three to Eight where you rated yourself on the five behaviors for each attribute. Now decide whether and how to change your ratings based on your expanded understanding and the self-reflection you've done throughout our time together. Note your new self-assessment here:

Farsighted	(1) Growth area (2) Strength (3) Key strength
Passionate	(1) Growth area (2) Strength (3) Key strength
Courageous	(1) Growth area (2) Strength (3) Key strength
Wise	(1) Growth area (2) Strength (3) Key strength
Generous	(1) Growth area (2) Strength (3) Key strength
Trustworthy	(1) Growth area (2) Strength (3) Key strength

This might also be a good time to turn to the Epilogue, where you'll find the instructions for obtaining your free online Accepted Leader self-assessment. It's more in-depth and rigorous than the approach I've suggested above, and you'll get an individualized summary report based on your ratings that will help you plan more effectively.

Play to Your Strength

Decide which of the six attributes is your greatest current strength. Rely not only on your own perceptions and beliefs about yourself, but also on what you've heard from any wizards, well-wishers, or other credible fair witnesses in your life. Once you've identified it, write in your notebook the attribute you believe is your greatest current strength.

Now think of three practical, day-to-day ways you can best use this strength to support your team and the success of your organization. You might want to review the chapter on this attribute. The five behaviors

and the developmental advice for each of them might be good thought starters for you, providing a framework for thinking about specific things you can start doing right now.

I've filled in two examples based on a current greatest strength of wise:

I'll use my key strength to:

> Help my team make objective decisions, especially in areas where we have a deep emotional stake

I'll use my key strength to:

> Do postmortems with my employees on key projects to look for patterns and decide how to improve going forward

Develop in Your Growth Areas

Referring once again to your new self-assessment, pick out the two growth area attributes where you believe you need the most development. One simple way to do this is to review your self-rating in the five behaviors for the attributes; the attributes for which you have the most 1s (a growth area) behaviors are probably your most important development areas. Then write in your notebook the two attributes you most want and need to work on developing.

In order to decide how to best develop in these areas, you're going to need some outside help. This is where the wizards, well-wishers, and wild cards come in handy.

Calling on Your Wizards

I'm assuming you already have a fairly clear idea of how you need to develop in both your growth area attributes given the advice and the "try it" activities you've already completed in the chapters about them. So let's focus on how to use your wizards to support that development. Think about and write down in your notebook what kind of help you'd like to ask for from the wizards in your life: your specific development need, whom to ask, and how to ask for it. To get you started, I've written out an example:

Growth area
   Generosity
Specific development need:
   sharing power and authority
Whom to ask:
   George—he's really good at delegation and is already a "wizard" for me
How I'll ask:
   Next time he and I have lunch, I'll share my assessment with him, tell him what I'm working on, and ask him to help me learn to delegate more consistently. I'll ask him how he got good at it, and if I can bounce situations off him to see whether I'm approaching them right.

Now work through this process for yourself. Decide on two "wizard requests" for each of your growth area attributes that you think will most help you develop.

Relying on Your Well-Wishers

Now let's take advantage of your well-wishers. I'd suggest you pick out your strongest well-wisher and let that person know that you'd like to share what you're working on and ask for his or her support. Here's a simple approach for doing that:

- *Provide context.* Let your well-wisher know that you're developing your leader capabilities, and provide an overview of the six attributes. Share your self-assessment. Then summarize the idea of needed supporters (wizards, well-wishers, and wild cards) and note that you see him or her as a well-wisher.

- *Explain what you're working on.* Share with your well-wisher what you've written above under "playing to your strength" and "developing in your growth areas."
- *Ask for his or her support.* Decide what you most need from this person and what you think he or she will be best at providing. It might simply be listening to your leadership aspirations and rooting for your success. You could ask for feedback about the feasibility or clarity of your plans. Or you may want this person to be your safety net: someone to turn to when you're feeling discouraged or overwhelmed on your journey to being a more effective leader and need someone to offer empathy and a hopeful voice. In your notebook, summarize the kind of support you'll ask for from your well-wisher.

Staying Alert for Wild Cards

Wild cards are by their very nature hard to predict or control. So I suggest that as you start to work your development plan—both on your own and with your wizard and well-wishers—keep your eyes and your mind open for people who seem to offer something that might help you develop in your growth areas. One of my favorite quotes is from Branch Rickey, a seminal figure in the development of American baseball; he broke the color barrier twice, by bringing both the first black player and the first Hispanic player into the major leagues, and he more or less invented the farm team system. When people would say that someone was "lucky," he would say, "Luck is the residue of design." In other words, what may look like luck to others is most often the result of careful planning. When you're clear in your intentions, you're better able to recognize opportunities that will support those intentions when they arise and take advantage of them.

It definitely applies to recognizing and taking advantage of wild cards in your leadership development journey: the clearer you get about what you most need to develop and what you have to offer as a leader, the more likely you'll be to recognize the potential of wild cards when they wander into your life.

As Our Story Ends . . . and Begins

Finally, I suggest you create an accurate, hopeful self-talk statement to support you in your leadership journey—one sentence that will remind you why you're working to become the kind of leader others want to follow and that it's possible for you to do so. You may want to write it in your trusty (and by this time, well-filled) *Leading* notebook, or you may even want to make yourself a small laminated card with your self-talk sentence on it that you can slip into your purse or wallet. Every time you read it, remember that young boy who started the *Leader* journey with little more than the clothes on his back, a will to succeed, and an open heart and mind. You too can become the leader people will follow.

Epilogue

If we were working together as coach and coachee, this is where I'd be walking you to the door, shaking your hand (or hugging you, if that's the kind of relationship we'd developed), wishing you well, and reconfirming when we'd next check in with each other.

Since I don't have that opportunity to interact with you in person, I'd like to offer to stay in touch in some other ways. First, you're welcome to follow either of my blogs. The one at erikaandersen.com is a personal take on leadership and learning, while my Forbes blog, at www.forbes.blogs.com/erikaandersen, is somewhat more structured and organization focused. I'd also love to invite you to become part of the conversation at the *Insider List,* a twice-monthly e-letter I send that offers both exclusive content and fresh ideas about leadership and work. You can opt into that at erikaandersen.com. And if you're interested in finding out more about the work my colleagues at Proteus and I do with our clients, check us out at www.proteus-international.com.

Finally, we have a gift for you. Because you've purchased the book, you can complete the Accepted Leader Assessment for free. You'll get an individualized report based on how you assess yourself in the six attributes I have focused on in this book. To get your free assessment, go to www.leadingsopeoplewillfollow.com, and type in your name, e-mail address, and the "secret word" as prompted onscreen in order to complete the assessment and get your individualized report.

Thank you much for giving me the opportunity to spend this time with you. I hope it has been useful and enjoyable in equal measure and that it has supported your highest intentions. May you become all that you want to become and make this world a better place.

Warmly,
Erika Andersen
April 2012

Listening and Self-Talk for Leaders: Bonus Section

Great leaders are excellent listeners, and they manage their self-talk. Because these two skills are key to developing all six leader attributes, I've included this bonus section to provide you with some in-depth guidance in both areas. What you learn here will support you in completing many of the activities offered through the book.

Listening

Listening is a developed skill, like tennis or carpentry. And like other skills, learning to do it well involves acquiring new behaviors. These are the listener ways of behaving, in a few words:

Listening Is

- Attending
- Inviting
- Questioning
- Restating

In this bonus section, I'll offer you ways to learn to do, or to get better at doing, these four things. I'll offer a practical explanation for everything

I recommend and encourage you to try it out in real life in a way that connects back to being an accepted leader.

Attending

The first skill of listening is so simple and obvious that we tend to underestimate its importance. However, paying attention to someone when he or she is speaking is the first effort you can make to keep the focus on that person.

These are the key elements of attending, or paying attention:

- *Physical focus:* making eye contact, turning toward the other person, not doing other tasks
- *Verbal focus:* not carrying on other conversations (even via e-mail or texting)
- *Mental focus:* making an effort to follow the other person's thinking and understand their feelings (versus daydreaming or thinking about what you're going to say when he or she takes a breath)

I'm sure this seems familiar to you: attending is simple and relatively easy to do. In fact, we all know how to do it, and we do it sometimes, usually when we're really interested in what the other person is saying or when we're creating a new relationship with someone who's important to us. All this makes it easy to underestimate its importance.

Think about the last time you were trying to talk about something you cared about to a person who wasn't paying attention. I had this experience last summer at a party. I was speaking with someone I'd just met, and he'd spent quite a while talking about himself. Then he said, "And what do you do?" I started to talk about my work, and within moments, he was looking at his watch, scanning the view behind me, smiling at others who walked by—pretty much not paying any attention to me at all. I just stopped talking. At one point he turned back to me, smiled brightly, and said, "Oh, that must be interesting," and started talking about himself again.

What impression do you suppose he made on me? And how do you imagine I would have felt about him if he'd been my new boss? Exactly. Not a great way to for him to demonstrate his fitness as a leader.

Although I already knew the power of this first listening skill, that little experience reinforced it for me.

Inviting

Attending, the first listening skill, is like being home when people come to visit. The next skill, inviting, is like opening the door and asking them to come in. Attending lets people know you're present; inviting encourages them to speak.

As with attending, inviting is something most people do automatically when they're relaxed and interested and when they have a good relationship with the person who's speaking. Bringing this skill to your conscious awareness gives you the option of using it to build better relationships of all kinds.

The skill of inviting has two key elements:

- *Physical gestures:* nodding, matching body language and expressions
- *Verbal gestures:* nonword sounds, encouraging phrases, brief questions that specifically encourage the speaker to begin or continue speaking

Here's how this looks and sounds. Let's say you're waiting for a meeting to begin and are talking to your boss's new boss, whom you've just met. As you speak, she stands facing you and nods in agreement. When you mention a project your team is working on, about which you're excited, she smiles with you and says, "Wow!" When you pause, wondering if she's getting bored, she asks, "So what's next?" And when you say that you're a little concerned about rolling it out to the other offices, she raises her eyebrows and nodding, says, "Mmmm. Tougher."

I suspect you would feel invited to keep talking.

Let's try the same scenario without the inviting. You're waiting for the meeting to begin, talking to your boss's new boss. As you speak, she looks at you but stands turned slightly away from you, arms folded. She seems a little distracted. When you mention a project your team is working on, about which you're excited, there's no change in her expression. When you pause, wondering if she's getting bored, she doesn't say anything. Losing steam and getting a bit uncomfortable, you add that you're a little concerned about rolling it out to the other offices. She stares at you blankly.

She's attending to you, but I don't imagine you feel invited to continue. You'd probably leave the first version of this conversation feeling respected and understood and the second feeling dismissed and embarrassed. After the first conversation, you'd probably have an initial impression of the boss's boss as an open, supportive person and a good leader. After the second version—not so much.

Like attending, inviting is a simple, almost invisible skill. And as in our scenario above, it can make the difference between creating an environment where others feel supported and encouraged to express their thoughts and ideas, and one where they don't.

Try It: Attending and Inviting

Sometime today, spend five minutes with your spouse, a friend, a colleague, or an employee simply attending and inviting while the other person talks about something that's important to him or her. Note the effect it has on the other person and on you. Note whether you hear more of what he or she says and whether he or she says something you haven't heard before.

As a leader, attending to and inviting those you lead while they're speaking is an immediate and powerful way to show your respect for and interest in them and to begin to find out more about who they are and what's important to them.

Questioning

Depending on how and why a question is asked, it can greatly hinder or greatly help the listening process. For instance, questions that focus on supporting your existing point of view get in the way of listening (for example, "Isn't distribution the main problem?" or "Couldn't you have addressed that sooner?"). They're just statements of what you already think, dressed up with a question mark. This kind of question forces the speaker to respond to your point of view rather than sharing his or her own.

Questions that support listening arise out of curiosity. They're an expression of your intention to find out the speaker's point of view (for example, "Do you see distribution as part of the problem?" or, "How could we have addressed that sooner?").

Here's a way to think about the differences between questions that hinder and those that foster listening:

Listening Questions	Nonlistening Questions
Information gathering	Information sharing
Curious	Directive
Asking for the speaker's point of view	Asserting a point of view

One of the best ways to tell what kind of question you're about to ask is to listen to the monologue inside your head. A curiosity-based question that focuses on finding out someone's point of view will tend to come from self-talk like, "Hmm, I wonder what she meant by that?" or "Now, that's interesting. I'd like to know more." In contrast, nonlistening questions tend to be preceded by self-talk like, "I don't agree. I think . . . ," or, "I need to set him straight."

Are you actively interested in hearing more about what the other person has to say? Do you want to hear it even if it contradicts your own opinions and ideas? Then your questions will probably have the characteristics of listening questions, as noted above: information gathering, curious, and asking for the speaker's point of view.

I'm not saying you shouldn't express a point of view. I'm just saying don't mush the two things together. When you're listening, listen. And when you want to express your point of view, just do it. Don't add a question mark at the end in order to pretend to be open-minded.

Try It: Questioning

Think of two people with whom you talk fairly regularly. The first person should be someone who puts you on the defensive—you often feel as though you're being asked to justify your point of view. The second person should be someone with whom you feel really comfortable—someone you feel accepts you as you are and is interested in hearing your point of view.

Next time you talk with each of these people, notice what kinds of questions they ask you: listening or nonlistening. I suspect you'll find that the person with whom you feel more comfortable tends to ask more listening questions.

Restating

The final skill of listening is the only one that for most people requires a conscious effort to learn. Unlike the first three, restating isn't something most of us already do. However, it's an extremely useful skill, particularly when you're trying to understand complex ideas, gather new information, or show the speaker that you understand him or her: all things good leaders need to do regularly. Restating is simply summarizing, in your own words, the essence of what the speaker has just said:

Restating Is

- In your own words
- The essence
- Only when needed

Restating completes a feedback loop between speaker and listener. Here's why that's important. We tend to assume that we understand what the other person is saying in a conversation; unfortunately, that's all too often not the case. How many times have you left a meeting or a conversation thinking that you and another person had the same understanding, only to find out later (after the packaging was orange and purple instead of blue, or nobody told the sales department what was expected of them, or the project went way over budget) just how wrong you were?

When you briefly restate the essence of the speaker's message in your own words, you're far less likely to have such frustrating (and expensive) misunderstandings. When your restatement is accurate, the speaker's reaction will often be, "Yes, exactly!" It's very gratifying, as the speaker, to know that the person listening really has understood you. Restating is both a great way to build connection and respect and a wonderfully quick and effective way to find out who people are and what's important to them.

So, how does restating sound? You might be thinking to yourself, "Won't it seem goofy if I just repeat what the other person has said?" But restating isn't just parroting back: it's capturing the core of what's been said, in your own words, and only when needed. (If someone says, "It's a nice day," you wouldn't say, "So, you think the weather is nice today." That *would* seem goofy.)

For example, an employee of yours might come into your office one day and say, "I don't want you to think I'm being negative, but I'm just not sure this new product is the right way to go. I know that part of your vision is to be more innovative, but this just seems too far away from our core expertise. I wish we could take the time to test it out better with some actual customers or potential customers. It just seems too rushed. It's a lot of time and money to put into something and then have it tank. Or maybe there has been testing, and I just don't know about it. I want to feel more confident we're doing the right thing."

Now instead of just leaping into fearless-leader-reassuring mode (remember, farsighted and passionate doesn't mean close-minded), you restate. You take a deep breath and say, "You're feeling conflicted about this. You're behind the push to be more innovative, but you're worried it could turn out badly without more thought or research." I suspect your employee would say something like, "Yes!" or "Exactly!" And as a result, you'd be sure that you understood his or her point of view before responding, and he or she would know you understood. Mutual clarity is a great starting point for any further conversation.

But what if your restatement doesn't capture the essence of what the other person has said? Does that mean you've failed? Not at all. Maybe after your succinct restatement, your employee says, "Well, kind of. I guess the thing I'm most worried about is that upper management will blame us if it turns out badly, even though they've said they want us to take more risks." Very interesting. That's a whole new level of information that you probably wouldn't have gotten to without restating.

So the good news is that restating is extremely valuable, even when your restatement is wrong, because it tends to keep moving the conversation toward greater clarity and deeper understanding of each other.

Yet another benefit is that your restatement invisibly requires your employee to reflect on his or her own words and take responsibility for what he or she is saying. After the conversation above, it would be easy for you, as the leader, to then say, "So how do you think we should handle this?" or, "Where do you think we should go next?" (great curiosity-based questions, by the way). Restating helps set up your employees to engage in solving problems and move toward the future with you instead of simply coming to you to be the solver of problems. It's a great way, in being farsighted, to invite others to participate in clarifying and achieving the vision. Passionate leaders use it to invite real dialogue. Wise leaders use restating to make sure they've accurately understood others' ideas or perspective, so they can assess situations objectively. You get the point: listening will support you in developing all of the leader attributes.

Managing Your Self-talk

Pretty much everyone has a continuous mental monologue running through their mind, like the "crawl" at the bottom of a TV screen. Sometimes what we say to ourselves is pretty benign ("I love oranges," "Great shoes," "It's hot today!"), but often it's not. Too often our mental monologue consists of unhelpful and inaccurate statements about ourselves and others ("That guy doesn't know anything," "I'm going to blow this presentation," "She hates me").

Learning to gain more control over how you talk to yourself is powerful for anyone, but especially helpful to leaders who are trying to build their leader capabilities. Managing your self-talk is particularly helpful in assessing the obstacles to your vision (farsightedness), taking responsibility for your actions (courage), and assessing situations objectively (wise).

Here are the steps:

- Recognize
- Record
- Revise
- Repeat

Recognize

The first step in managing your self-talk is to hear it. Most of the time, our little interior commentator runs and runs, and we're not even consciously aware that we're talking to ourselves, much less exactly what we're saying. Unless you're aware of this internal monologue, it's impossible to change it. So first you need to simply recognize what you're saying to yourself. For instance, let's say you're thinking about possible obstacles to the future you've envisioned. You might hear your mental voice saying, "There are so many reasons this won't happen. I should just give up." Or your particular self-talk might be exactly the opposite: "Whoever says this is a bad idea is just shortsighted and negative. It's the best idea ever!" Once you start attending to the voice in your head, you might be very surprised at what you're saying to yourself.

Record

Writing down your self-talk is an important part of managing it, particularly if it's something you've said to yourself repeatedly over a long period of time (most of us have a few of these unhelpful mental tape loops). Recording your self-talk creates a useful separation. When you see it written down, your internal monologue feels less like an intrinsic part of you. Let's say you write down that first self-talk statement above: "There are so many reasons this won't happen. I should just give up." Having written it down, you may see it differently. The first time I saw a piece of my own negative self-talk in writing, my immediate reaction was, *That's what I've been thinking? Yikes. I don't want to say that to myself. I don't even believe it's true!* Once you recognize and record it, you'll also be better able to look objectively at how this negative self-talk affects you. Perhaps it makes you more likely to abandon goals that are important to you, or to feel cynical or hopeless about the possibility of changing a bad situation.

Revise

After you've recorded inaccurate, unsupportive self-talk, you can decide how to rethink it. This step is the core of the process. You want to create alternative self-talk that you'll believe and that will lead to a more appropriate response. For instance, if you try to substitute self-talk that's falsely positive, like, "There are no obstacles. Nothing can stop us," you simply won't believe it, and therefore it will have no impact on you: you'll just revert back to your original negative self-talk. What could you say to yourself that's believable and that would create a more useful response? How about something like: "I know there are reasons this might not work. I'll look at them carefully, so I have the best chance of understanding and overcoming them."

Repeat

Like any other habit, managing your self-talk requires repetition. Substituting more hopeful and accurate self-talk for your negative self-talk will be helpful the very first time you do it. *And* you'll need to consciously do it again the next time the voice in your head comes up with a similarly unhelpful statement. And again. This is a process for creating new habits of thought. Whenever you find yourself falling into a pattern of unhelpful self-talk, either overly negative or overly positive, consciously substitute your revised, more realistic, accurate self-talk.

I encourage you to return to whatever chapter you were on when you started reading this, so you can incorporate your new understanding of listening and self-talk into all your leading behaviors.

Acknowledgments

First and foremost, I acknowledge all the excellent leaders I've known and worked with over the years who *aren't* mentioned in the book. I feel honored every day to work with all of you, and I learn at least as much from you as you do from me. Thank you for allowing all of us at Proteus to support you and share in your success.

I also thank the book team, without whom none of this would be happening. Jim Levine is my literary agent extraordinaire, whose personal and professional commitment to each of my books has been heartening and motivating from day one. And to Susan Williams, my wise and savvy editor at Jossey-Bass: I wanted to work with you from our first conversation, and here we are. Thank you so much for championing this work. For Barbara Henricks of Cave Henricks Communications and Rusty Shelton of Shelton Interactive: I believe you're the best in the business, and I'm thrilled, as always, to have you with us on the team. Sue Gebelein, I'm so glad Jeff found you: the assessment process could not have happened without you. And Dan, so happy to have you as my wingman and social media point person.

Jeff: Thank you. I love building this business with you and can't imagine a better partner. It's getting more and more interesting as we figure out how we want to do this and how we can be most helpful to people. Here's to the next however many years.

My fellow Proteans: We're all going to have fun with this one. I'm so grateful to be working with each and every one of you.

To my wonderful kids (that includes you, Katey) and their families: Being your parent has made and continues to make me a better person, a better leader, and a better thinker. Consider this a handbook for the leadership roles I know that each of you will have throughout your lives.

Patrick: Every single hour of every single day: home.

The Author

Since 1980, Erika Andersen has developed a reputation for creating approaches to learning and business building that are custom tailored to her clients' challenges, goals, and culture. She and her colleagues at Proteus International focus uniquely on leader readiness, supporting leaders at all levels to get ready and stay ready to meet whatever the future might bring.

Much of her recent work has focused on organizational visioning and strategy, executive coaching, and management and leadership development. In these capacities, she serves as consultant and adviser to the CEOs and top executives of a number of corporations, including NBC Universal, Gannett Corporation, Rockwell Automation, Turner Broadcasting, GE, Union Square Hospitality Group, and Madison Square Garden.

She also shares her insights about managing people and creating successful businesses by speaking to corporations, nonprofit groups, and national associations. Her books and learning guides have been translated into Spanish, Turkish, German, French, Russian, and Chinese, and she has been quoted in a variety of national publications, including the *Wall Street Journal, Fortune,* and the *New York Times.* Andersen is one of the most popular business bloggers at Forbes.com. She is the author of *Growing Great Employees: Turning Ordinary People into Extraordinary Performers* (Portfolio, 2006) and *Being Strategic: Plan for Success; Outthink Your Competitors; Stay Ahead of Change* (St. Martin's Press, May 2009) and the author and host of *Being Strategic with Erika Andersen* on public television.

Index

Page references followed by *fig* indicate an illustrated figure.

Now that you've read *Leading So People Will Follow*, you might want to know more about how my colleagues and I work with our clients. Proteus is a team of smart, passionate, honorable folks who bring to life the skills and ideas in my books, blogs, and TV show. All the work we do focuses on leader readiness: we help leaders *get ready and stay ready for whatever the future might bring*. We work in three practice areas:

STRENGTHENING LEADERS

We draw upon the model at the heart of *Leading So People Will Follow*, as well as the ideas and skills in *Growing Great Employees* and *Being Strategic*, to support leaders to be more fully accepted and to better build their business. We coach leaders individually and in teams.

CLARIFYING VISION AND STRATEGY

This is where we put our approach—outlined in the *Being Strategic* book and television show—into practice. We work with companies of all sizes and types to envision a successful organizational future, to craft a practical plan for getting there, and to engage their people in making it a reality.

BUILDING SKILLS AND KNOWLEDGE

Growing Great Employees provides clear guidance about why and how to manage well. We offer powerful, practical training programs based on the skills in this book, so that people leave our courses ready and able to manage and lead better. And we can teach our clients' trainers to get the same results.

If you'd like to find out how we might help you and your company to get ready and stay ready for your own future, please feel free to email us at connect@proteus-international.com or call 888.926.9627 (+1 212.830.9870 from outside the United States). Thanks very much for your interest.